Medical Investigation 101 Workbook

Interactive Assignments to Reinforce and Challenge Your New Medical Knowledge

Aligned to *Medial Investigation 101: A Book to Inspire Your Interest in Medicine and How Doctors Think*

by

Dr. Russ Hill

Dr. Richard Griffith

Illustrations by Raella Hill

Copyright ©2017 Hill & Griffith

All Rights Reserved

No part of this workbook may be reproduced in any form or by any electronic or mechanical means, including information storage and retrieval systems, without permission in writing from the publisher, except by reviewers, who may quote brief passages in a review.

Written and Published by

Dr. Russ Hill

Laguna Beach, California

and

Dr. Richard Griffith

Guilford, Vermont

Artwork images by Raella Hill

Laguna Beach, California

Table of Contents

Workbook Introduction		1
Introduction to Medical Investigation		2
Investigation 1.1,	Types of Medical Doctors	6
Investigation 1.2,	Medical Support Team	17
Investigation 2.0/2.1,	Medical Diagnostic Process, Chief Complaint	26
Investigation 2.2,	Medical History	31
Investigation 2.3/2.4,	Review of Systems & Medical Exam	36
Investigation 2.5/2,	Differential Diagnosis & Diagnosis	45
Investigation 2.7,	SOAP Notes	50
Investigation 3.1A,	Breathing Difficulty	57
Investigation 3.1B,	Pulmonary Embolism	62
Investigation 3.2A,	Abdominal Pain	67
Investigation 3.2B,	Microbes	75
Investigation 3.3A,	Rib Area Pain	86
Investigation 3.3B,	Shingles	95
Investigation 3.4A,	Sore Throat	100
Investigation 3.4B,	Role of Blood	106
Investigation 3.5A,	Emergencies	114
Investigation 3.5B,	Chest Pain	122
Investigation 3.6A,	Chronic Disease	130
Investigation 3.6B,	Diabetes	139
Investigation 3.7A,	Shoulder Pain	148
Investigation 3.7B,	Joints	154
Investigation 3.8A,	Fever & Cough	160
Investigation 3.8B,	Respiratory System	169
Investigation 3.9A,	Abdominal Pain & Dark Urine	176
Investigation 3.9B,	Urinary Tract	184
Investigation 3.10A,	Weak & Dizzy	191
Investigation 3.10B,	Environmental Toxins	203
Investigation 3.11A,	Foodborne Illness	208
Investigation 3.11B,	Case Study, Foodborne Illness	214
Investigation 3.12A,	Head Injury	223

Investigation 3.12B,	The Eye	226
Investigation 3.13A,	The Brain	232
Investigation 3.13B,	Normal or Abnormal	244
Investigation 3.14A/B,	Final Case/Circle of Life	250
Investigation 3.15,	Looking Deeper	257
Post-Script		261
About the Authors		262
Certificate of Achievement		264

Workbook Introduction

Welcome to the *Medical Investigation 101 Workbook*. This workbook aligns with and supplements the material from *Medical Investigation 101*. It provides opportunities to reinforce and measure your learning from each chapter. The more medical terminology you master, and the more you understand about medical investigation, the better your preparation for future encounters with healthcare providers. Understanding how to transfer techniques for solving medical investigations to your analysis of decisions you make in your everyday life will serve you well. Understanding treatment modalities on the horizon can help you ask better questions and make better decisions when treatment options are discussed with your own physician. Should you find yourself pondering healthcare career choices, realizing the myriad of options may provide some light at the end of that tunnel.

The workbook includes assignments for each chapter and includes vocabulary research, reinforcing word match, and crossword puzzle. Assignments related to chapter content help galvanize important information and concepts. Extending activities provide an opportunity to think deeper and outside the box.

We encourage teachers to utilize the materials to foster improved medical terminology vocabulary and understanding of the healthcare system in all students. Whether students already demonstrate interest in healthcare careers, or simply care about how to communicate effectively with their physicians, everyone should find something of value in the material.

Thank you for choosing to enhance your *Medical Investigation 101* by utilizing this workbook. We hope you find it useful.

Introduction   Dr._____

Assignment 1: **Vocabulary**   P._____ Date:_____

Directions: Use the text, a dictionary, or the internet to write a definition for each term.

1. physician: _____
   _____

2. pediatrician: _____
   _____

3. specialist: _____
   _____

4. diagnosis: _____
   _____

5. treatment: _____
   _____

6. art of medical practice: _____
   _____

7. science of medical practice: _____
   _____

8. physiology: _____
   _____

9. pathophysiology: _____
   _____

10. pathologist: _____
    _____

11. history: _____
    _____

12. symptoms: _____
    _____

13. abnormal: _____

14. fracture: _____

Introduction

Assignment 2: Vocabulary Match

Dr._____

P._____ Date:_____

Directions: Write the letter of the definition at the right next to the medical term on the left in the space provided.

1. _____ physician
2. _____ pediatrician
3. _____ specialist
4. _____ diagnosis
5. _____ treatment
6. _____ art of medical practice
7. _____ science of medical practice
8. _____ physiology
9. _____ pathophysiology
10. _____ pathologist
11. _____ history
12. _____ symptoms
13. _____ abnormal
14. _____ fracture

a. A specialist who often examines tissue under a microscope
b. Dealing with patients in a caring and forgiving manner
c. A feeling or bodily feature that suggests illness or injury
d. Physician who cares for children
e. Details about how the human body normally works
f. A break in a bone
g. The cause of the problem
h. How illness or injury makes the body work abnormally
i. Doctor who treats only specific illnesses or parts of the body
j. The opposite of normal
k. Medical doctor or practitioner
l. The patient's story about how their health has changed
m. A session of medical care using a drug or physical action
n. Scientific knowledge of chemistry, physics, anatomy, physiology & pathophysiology

Introduction Dr._____

Vocabulary Assignment 3: Sentences P.____ Date:_____

Directions: Use each word in a complete sentence.

1. physician: _____
_____

2. pediatrician: _____
_____

3. specialist: _____
_____

4. diagnosis: _____
_____

5. treatment: _____
_____

6. art of medical practice: _____
_____

7. science of medical practice: _____
_____

8. physiology: _____
_____

9. pathophysiology: _____
_____

10. pathologist: _____
_____

11. history: _____
_____

12. symptoms: _____
_____

13. abnormal: _____

14. fracture: _____

Investigation 1.0 - Introduction
Crossword 1.0

Dr._____
P.____Date:_____

Medical Investigation

Directions: Use the highlighted terms in the chapter to solve the puzzle. Most clues come from the chapter text, but some require outside investigation. Omit spaces or dashes between words.

ACROSS

1. finding the cause of the health problem
2. the name of the book
3. the changes in one's health that cause us to look for the cause
5. the part of medical practice requiring knowledge of chemistry, physics, physiology, pathophysiology, and anatomy
7. doctors who treat only children
8. the details about how the human body normally works
9. another name for medical doctors
10. a solution to make the patient feel better
13. a method doctors use to add to what they know about a patient
15. the patient's story about how their health has changed

DOWN

1. the cause of the problem
4. an important skill utilized to find clues that help make the diagnosis
6. the details of how human body function goes wrong
7. the Greek word meaning a feeling or illness
11. the part of medical practice that incorporates a sense within the practitioner of human nature and a will to deal with fellow humans in a caring and forgiving manner
12. the opposite of normal
14. used to find a bone fracture

Investigation 1.1   Dr._____

Types of Medical Doctors   P._____ Date:_____

Vocabulary Assignment 1A: Definitions

Directions: Use the text, a dictionary, or the internet to define these terms:

1. cardiologist: _____
   _____

2. sub-specialty: _____
   _____

3. catheter: _____
   _____

4. invasive cardiology: _____
   _____

5. gerontologist: _____
   _____

6. tipping point: _____
   _____

7. artificial intelligence: _____
   _____

8. hybrid thinking: _____
   _____

9. lifelong learning: _____
   _____

10. residency program: _____
    _____

11. fellowship: _____
    _____

12. cardiothoracic surgeon: _____
    _____

Investigation 1.1 Dr._____

Types of Medical Doctors P._____ Date:_____

Vocabulary Assignment 1B: Definitions

Directions: Use the text, a dictionary, or the internet to define these terms:

1. neurosurgeon: _____
   _____

2. orthopedic surgeon: _____
   _____

3. emergency physician: _____
   _____

4. pediatrician: _____
   _____

5. oncologist: _____
   _____

6. hematologist: _____
   _____

7. nephrologist: _____
   _____

8. otolaryngologist: _____
   _____

9. dermatologist: _____
   _____

10. anesthesiologist: _____
    _____

11. toxicologist: _____
    _____

12. podiatrist: _____
    _____

Investigation 1.1

Types of Medical Doctors

Dr._____

P._____ Date:_____

Vocabulary Assignment 2: Matching #1

Directions: Write the letter of the definition at the right next to the medical term on the left in the space provided.

1. _____ cardiologist
2. _____ sub-specialty
3. _____ catheter
4. _____ invasive cardiologists
5. _____ gerontologist
6. _____ tipping point
7. _____ artificial intelligence
8. _____ hybrid thinking
9. _____ lifelong learning
10. _____ residency program
11. _____ fellowship
12. _____ cardiothoracic surgeon

a. Cardiologists who thread small tubes through veins into the heart
b. Training to become a sub-specialist
c. Programming computers to mimic the thought processes of humans
d. Example: an Orthopedic Surgeon who treats only knee problems
e. Treats severe injuries to the chest requiring surgery
f. Type of learning required of physicians
g. Small tube inserted into a vein and threaded to the heart
h. Physician treating only the elderly
i. Blending computer processing with human skills to solve problems
j. The point at which small changes bring about a totally new solution
k. Physician treating only heart related problems
l. Training to become a specialist

Investigation 1.1　　　　　　　　　　　Dr._____

Types of Medical Doctors　　　　　　　P._____ Date:_____

Vocabulary Assignment 2: Matching #2

Directions: Write the letter of the definition at the right next to the medical term on the left in the space provided.

1. _____ emergency physician　　　　　a. Provides surgery pain-free
2. _____ pediatrician　　　　　　　　　b. Treats only newborns
3. _____ oncologist　　　　　　　　　　c. Treats cancer
4. _____ pathologist　　　　　　　　　　d. Studies chemical exposure
5. _____ nephrologist　　　　　　　　　e. Treats kidney diseases
6. _____ otolaryngologist　　　　　　　f. Triages patients with acute illness
7. _____ dermatologist　　　　　　　　　　or injury
8. _____ anesthesiologist　　　　　　　g. Expert in cosmetic surgery
9. _____ toxicologist　　　　　　　　　h. Treats only mental illness
10. _____ podiatrist　　　　　　　　　　i. Treats skin lesions
11. _____ plastic surgeon　　　　　　　j. Treats respiratory tract problems
12. _____ pulmonologist　　　　　　　　k. Treats only children
13. _____ neonatologist　　　　　　　　l. Treats only foot & ankle injuries
14. _____ psychiatrist　　　　　　　　　m. Treats ears, nose & throat

　　　　　　　　　　　　　　　　　　　　n. Examines tissue under microscope & performs chemical tests to diagnose disease

Investigation 1.1 Dr._____

Types of Medical Doctors P._____ Date:_____

Vocabulary Assignment 3B-1: Sentences

Directions: Write a complete sentence using each vocabulary term below.

1. specialty: _____

2. sub-specialty: _____

3. catheter: _____

4. invasive cardiology: _____

5. primary care: _____

6. tipping point: _____

7. artificial intelligence: _____

8. hybrid thinking: _____

9. lifelong learning: _____

10. residency program: _____

11. fellowship: _____

12. cardiothoracic surgeon: _____

Investigation 1.1   Dr._____

Types of Medical Doctors   P._____ Date:_____

Vocabulary Assignment 3B-2: Sentences

Directions: Write a complete sentence using each vocabulary term below.

1. neurosurgeon: _____
   _____

2. orthopedic surgeon: _____
   _____

3. emergency physician: _____
   _____

4. pediatrician: _____
   _____

5. oncologist: _____
   _____

6. hematologist: _____
   _____

7. nephrologist: _____
   _____

8. otolaryngologist: _____
   _____

9. dermatologist: _____
   _____

10. anesthesiologist: _____
    _____

11. toxicologist: _____
    _____

12. podiatrist: _____
    _____

Investigation 1.1

Dr._____

Medical Specialties Worksheet

P.____Date_____

Directions: Identify on the right side of the chart the area of expertise for each specialist on the left.

Physician Specialty	What types of problems or patients do they treat?
Gerontologist	
Oncologist	
Dermatologist	
Otolaryngologist	
Internist	
Psychiatrist	
Orthopedist	
Anesthesiologist	
Pediatrician	
Hematologist	
Obstetrician	
Cardiologist	
Neurologist	
Pathologist	
Toxicologist	
Infectious Diseases	
Gastroenterologist	
Plastic Surgeon	
Neonatologist	
Podiatrist	
Ophthalmologist	
Acupuncturist	
Dentist	
Pulmonologist	
Family Practice	

Investigation 1.1   Dr._____

Worksheet 1.1.5   P._____ Date:_____

Types of Physicians: Referrals

Since human minds find the human body quite complex, a single doctor cannot possibly treat every type of medical problem. Physicians routinely call on other doctors to help them when they feel that doctor can do a better job of solving the problem for the patient. When this happens it is called **referring** the patient.

In this activity **YOU** are the Family Practitioner. When patients come to you with problems you can easily solve, you take care of the patient yourself. But when you cannot confidently make a diagnosis on your patient's complaints you would refer that patient to another physician who has more experience with that type of problem.

What does it mean to "refer" the patient?

_____

In each situation below, to which physician would you most likely refer the patient?

1. A 45 year old male patient complains of ringing in their ears which has been present on and off for two months. You find no obvious reason for this, so you decide to refer the patient to a specialist. To which specialist would you probably send this patient?

    Patient 1: _____

2. An 87 year old female is brought to you by her daughter because she goes for walks and get lost in her own neighborhood. She likes to drive her car but has trouble remembering where she parked it. The elderly lady constantly asks you the same question over and over. To which specialist would you probably refer this patient?

    Patient 2: _____

3. The mother of a thirteen year old boy brings him into your office. She tells you her son fell off his skateboard while doing ramp jumping in the back yard. She believes he injured his left arm. You look at the arm and find the arm has swollen and the boy reports it feels very tender to the touch. You order an x-ray, which shows a break in the radius bone of the lower arm.
    a. Which bone do we call the radius? LARGER or SMALLER bone of the forearm (Circle the correct answer)
    b. To which doctor would you refer this patient for further evaluation and treatment?
       Patient 3:_____

Investigation 1.1

Worksheet 1.1B.5, page 2

Dr._____

P.____ Date:_____

4. A 57 year old man comes to you because he is concerned that he occasionally feels light headed and gets dizzy. He cannot tell you any particular activity that causes this to happen. When you listen to his heart you hear an irregular heart beat and an abnormal sloshing sound between the normal beats of the heart.

   To which physician specialist might you consider referring this patient?

   Patient 4:_____

5. A 21 year old female comes to your office complaining she always feels weak and tired. She says she sometimes sees black spots in her field of vision and occasionally experiences difficulty keeping her balance. You take a blood sample and look at it under the microscope. You find an abnormally low number of red blood cells.
   a. What important substance do red blood cells carry?

   _____

   b. To which specialist would you probably refer this patient?

   Patient 5: _____

6. A 35 year old female comes to you complaining of pain and numbness starting in her right hip and shooting down her right leg. Lifting heavy objects makes the pain worse and the pain has been growing progressively worse over the past several months. On examination you find the patient cannot feel sharpness on the skin of the right leg when touched with a sharp probe and cannot feel the difference between a warm and cold wet gauze when applied to the right leg.

   To which physician would you refer this patient?
   Patient 6: _____

7. A Mother brings in a nine year old girl after her pet cat scratched the girl's face. The mother is concerned the child might catch cat scratch fever. When you examine the wound you see a deep cut on the right cheek below the eye that goes deep enough to require stitches. You write a prescription for an antibiotic to protect the child from cat scratch fever, but you decide to refer the girl to a specialist for her stitches because very small, careful stitches may prevent her from developing a noticeable scar on her face.

   Who would you refer this patient to for facial stitches?

   Patient 7: _____

Investigation 1.1.6   Dr._____

Crossword: Medical Specialties   P.____ Date:_____

Directions: Use the highlighted terms in the chapter to solve the puzzle. Most clues come from the chapter text, but some require outside investigation. Omit spaces or dashes between words.

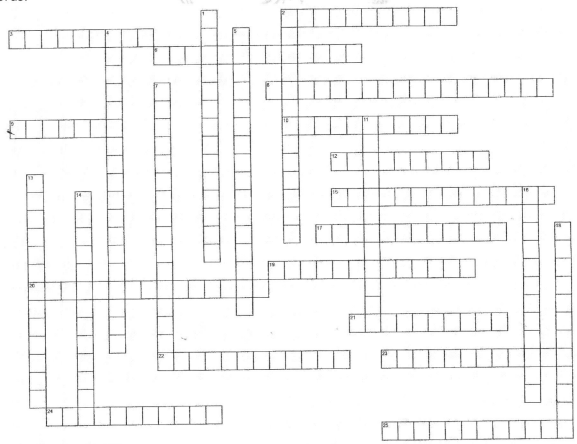

ACROSS

2 evaluates and treats nerve injuries and nerve related disorders
3 evaluates and treats adult conditions of the internal organs
6 specialist in evaluating and treating diseases and conditions of the lungs
8 evaluates and treats probles of the stomach and intestines
9 evaluates and treats conditions of the teeth and gums
10 evaluates and treats injuries and disorders of bones and joints
12 evaluates and treats injures and deformities of the foot
15 evaluates and treats surgically injuries and deformities of skin or soft tissue
17 diagnoses and treats neuromuscular disorders uing manual adjustment and manipulation of the spine
19 practices a component of Chinese medicine where thin needles are inserted into the body
20 evaluates and treat injuries and diseases of the eye
21 diagnoses and treats cancer
22 evaluates and treats conditions related to dangerous chemicals in our bodies
23 evaluates and treats heart conditions
24 examines tissue under a microscope and performs chemical tests to diagnose disease
25 evaluates and treats blood disorders

DOWN

1 evaluates and treats basic medical problems of children and adults; refers complex problems to specialists
2 evaluates and treats only newborn babies
4 evaluates and treats infections and contagious diseases
5 helps patients undergo surgery without pain; evaluates and treats pain
7 evaluates and treats conditions of the ears, nose, and throat
11 evaluates and treats only children
13 evaluates and treat skin disorders
14 evaluates and treats the elderly
16 delivers babies
18 evaluates and treats mental conditions

Investigation 1.1.7

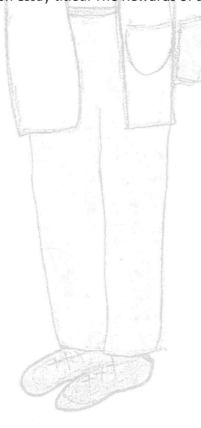

Extension Activities:

1. Write a paragraph about what you think might be your greatest challenges to becoming a doctor.

2. Write a paragraph about your opinion of the greatest challenge for you in working as a doctor.

3. Write a paragraph about what you think would be the greatest reward to working as a physician.

4. If you were to become a doctor, what type of doctor would you want to be and why?

5. Write a five paragraph essay titled: Three Types of Doctor I Would Most Like to Be

6. Write a five paragraph essay titled: The Rewards of a Working as a Medical Doctor?

Investigation 1.2 Dr. _____

Medical Support Team P.____ Date_____

Vocabulary Assignment 1: Definitions

Directions: Use the text, a dictionary, or the internet to write a definition for each term below.

1. receptionist: _____
_____

2. registered nurse: _____
_____

3. physician assistant: _____
_____

4. nurse practitioner: _____
_____

5. physical therapist: _____
_____

6. optometrist: _____
_____

7. speech therapist: _____
_____

8. dental hygienist: _____
_____

9. pharmacist: _____
_____

10. occupational therapist: _____
_____

11. psychologist: _____
_____

12. chiropractor: _____
_____

Investigation 1.2

Medical Support Team

Vocabulary Assignment 1: Definitions

Dr. _____

P. _____ Date _____

Directions: Write the letter of the definition at the right next to the medical term on the left in the space provided.

1. _____ receptionist
2. _____ registered nurse
3. _____ physician assistant
4. _____ nurse practitioner
5. _____ physical therapist
6. _____ optometrist
7. _____ speech therapist
8. _____ dental hygienist
9. _____ pharmacist
10. _____ occupational therapist
11. _____ psychologist
12. _____ chiropractor

a. specially qualified to prepare and dispense medicinal drugs
b. helps patients reduce pain and improve or restore mobility
c. greets patients and sets up appointments
d. studies mental processes and human behavior by observing, interpreting, and recording how people relate to one another
e. performs diagnosis and manipulative treatment of misalignments of the spine
f. helps those having speech difficulties and language issues
g. treats patients under supervision of a physician, but not a nurse
h. rehabilitates patients to perform daily and work related activities
i. a registered nurse (RN) with advanced training in diagnosing and treating illness
j. examines eyes, prescribes glasses & contact lenses, treats eye infections
k. Carries out treatment plans order by physicians & monitors patients' progress
l. Cleans teeth, assesses for oral diseases, & provides preventive care under supervision of dentist

Investigation 1.2: Medical Support Team   Dr. _____

Vocabulary 3: Sentences   P._____ Date_____

Directions: Use each medical career below in a complete sentence.

1. receptionist: _____
   _____

2. registered nurse: _____
   _____

3. physician assistant: _____
   _____

4. nurse practitioner: _____
   _____

5. physical therapist: _____
   _____

6. optometrist: _____
   _____

7. speech therapist: _____
   _____

8. dental hygienist: _____
   _____

9. pharmacist: _____
   _____

10. occupational therapist: _____
    _____

11. psychologist: _____
    _____

12. chiropractor: _____
    _____

Investigation 1.2
Worksheet 1.2.4

Dr._____
P.____Date:_____

Medical Support Team Members

Medical Support Team Member   **How they help Doctors & Patients**

Medical Support Team Member	How they help Doctors & Patients
Pharmacist	
Dental Hygienist	
Registered Nurse (RN)	
Massage Therapist	
Surgical Technician	
Phlebotomist	
Optometrist	
Orthopedic Technician	
Respiratory Therapist	
Cardiology Technician	
Medical Librarian	
Radiology Technician	
Occupational Therapist	
Medical Records Clerk	
Nuclear Medicine Tech	
Dental Assistant	
Speech Therapist	
Chiropractor	
Audiologist	
Nurse Practitioner	
Clinical Psychologist	
Physical Therapist	
Ultrasound Technician	

Investigation 1.2 Dr._____

1.2.5: Medical Support Team Referrals P._____ Date:_____

Physicians diagnose the problem causing the patient's complaint and decide which treatments will help most. Since doctors often don't have the time or equipment necessary to administer the treatment themselves, they often refer the patient to a member of the Medical Support Team. For example, if you have a sore throat with a cough and green phlegm, the doctor might write a prescription for antibiotic pills. Most physicians do not keep all the medicines they prescribe in their office; instead they send you to a member of the support team that knows all about prescription medicines, called a Pharmacist.

Directions:

In this activity **YOU are the Family Practitioner**. When patients come to you with common problems where you know the answer but don't have what they need, you can refer them to the appropriate medical support team member. Your challenge here is to refer your patients to the appropriate support team member so they get the best results. **Select your answers from the support team members listed in Worksheet 1.2A and record your answers on the following pages.**

Investigation 1.2 Dr._____

Worksheet 1.2.5 P.____ Date:_____

The Medical Support Team

Directions: Write the medical support team member who might best assist the patient and the physician in each situation.

Patient 1 is an 11 year old female who fell on her right wrist playing soccer. She felt immediate pain in the area and was brought to you for evaluation and treatment. An x-ray showed a small fracture, or break, in one of the bones of her wrist. She was placed in a cast for six weeks and the cast removed. Another x-ray showed the fracture healing well. The girl complained that her wrist was stiff and weak. You wrote her a prescription to visit which support team member?

Patient 1: _____

Patient 2 is a 19 year old male who visits your office with a complaint of bad breath. You ask him if he has been to a dentist in the past year; his reply is : "No". When you look in his mouth you notice a small amount of redness (erythema) in his gums. You recommend a visit to a dentist as soon as possible. The Dentist examines his teeth and notes small pieces of rotten food between some of his teeth in addition to the erythema in his gum tissue. No cavities are found on the examination. Who would the Dentist refer this patient to for treatment?

Patient 2: _____

Patient 3 is a 63 year old female who visits your office with a complaint that her husband always accuses her of saying "What did you say?" "He thinks I can't hear him when he speaks; but I think he is just mumbling." You perform a simple hearing test and observe that her hearing appears to be affected in her left ear. You examine her for excess ear wax and find none. At this point you might consider referring this lady for further evaluation, but to whom?

Patient 3: _____

Patient 4 is a 62 year old male who has been your patient for many years. About four months ago he suffered a stroke which left him with great difficulty speaking. You would like him to get help so that he can regain some of his speaking skills. Which medical support team member would you refer him to?

Patient 4: _____

Investigation 1.2
Worksheet 1.2.5, page 2

Dr._____
P._____ Date:_____

Patient 5 is a 73 year old male smoker who has been admitted to the hospital with difficulty breathing. Because he has smoked for over 50 years he has a previous diagnosis of emphysema. When you listen to the sounds coming from his lungs using your stethoscope you hear sounds consistent with pneumonia. Which medical support team member would you call on to help this patient breath more comfortably?

      Patient 5: _____

Patient 6 is a 51 year old male who visits you complaining of intermittent chest pain, which usually goes away when he stops walking or being active. Right now his chest does not hurt. Your testing machine is broken, so you refer him to the hospital to have an EKG test. Which member of the hospital support team would most likely perform this test on your patient?

      Patient 6: _____

Patient 7 is a 39 year old female who has recently returned from a trip to Africa. She complains of intermittent fever and chills, and a lack of appetite. You want to know more about the current diseases occurring in Africa. Which member of the support team could help find the information so you can know the most likely diseases to consider?

      Patient 7: _____

Patient 8 is a 24 year old pregnant female wanting to attempt to determine the sex of her unborn baby. Which member of the support team could perform an ultrasound test that might provide that information?

      Patient 8: _____

Investigation 1.2

Dr._____

Crossword 1.2.6: Medical Support Team

P.____ Date:_____

Directions: Use the highlighted terms in the chapter to solve the puzzle. Most clues come from the chapter text, but some require outside investigation. Omit spaces or dashes between words.

ACROSS

4 Carry out physician treatment plan; monitor care of very sick patients, supervise LVNs & LNAs
7 Administers heart related tests such as EKG and stress tests
9 Re-teach patients basic life skills in rehabilitation from serious injury or disease
12 Relax tight muscles and relieve stress by stretching and manipulating muscles
14 A nurse who works under the supervision of a registered nurse
19 Perform eye examinations and dispense glasses and contact lenses
20 Assist surgeons in the operating room and care for surgical instruments
21 Take blood samples from patients for testing

DOWN

1 Administers breathing treatments to patients as directed by physician
2 Sets up continuing education programs for doctors and nurses
3 Administers ultrasound tests for pregnant women and other tests as directed by physicians
5 Takes x-rays and administers MRI tests as directed by physician
6 Works with doctors and nurses to keep all patient medical records organized
7 Diagnose and treat mental, emotional, and behavioral disorders
8 Prepare radioactive drugs and administer to patients having special tests
10 Researches articles and new information for physicians
11 Assists Orthopedic Surgeon in surgery and applies and removes casts
13 Evaluates and treats patinets with speech problems
15 prepares and handles dental instruments and materials; assists dentist in treating patients
16 Dispense prescribed and over-the-counter medicines, check for drug interactins, give vaccine shots
17 Examine teeth and gums for dentist, clean teeth and gums
18 Evaluates and treats hearing problems

Investigation 1.2 Dr._____

Investigation 1.2.7 P._____Date:_____

Additional Activities:

1. Write a paragraph about what you think might be your greatest challenges to becoming a healthcare support team member.

2. Write a paragraph about your opinion of the greatest challenge for you in working in a medical support team role.

3. Write a paragraph about what you think would be the greatest rewards to working as a medical support team member.

4. If you were to become a medical support team member, which role would you want to fill and why?

5. Write a five paragraph essay titled: Three Medical Support Members I Would Most Like to Be

6. Write a five paragraph essay titled: The Rewards of a Career in Healthcare?

Investigation 2.0/2.1   Dr. _____

Medical Examination/Chief Complaint   P._____ Date _____

Vocabulary 1: Definitions

Directions: Use the book or internet to write a definition for each medical term below.

1. subjective findings: _____
   _____

2. objective findings: _____
   _____

3. diagnosis: _____
   _____

4. scientific method: _____
   _____

5. art of medicine: _____
   _____

6. chief complaint: _____
   _____

7. secondary complaints: _____
   _____

8. exacerbate: _____
   _____

9. symptoms: _____
   _____

10. acute: _____
    _____

11. chronic: _____
    _____

12. differential diagnosis: _____
    _____

Investigation 2.0/2.1　　　　　　　　　　　　　　　Dr. _____

Medical Examination/Chief Complaint　　　　　　P._____ Date_____

Vocabulary 2: Matching

Directions: Write the letter of the definition at the right next to the medical term on the left in the space provided.

1. _____ subjective findings
2. _____ objective findings
3. _____ diagnosis
4. _____ scientific method
5. _____ art of medicine
6. _____ chief complaint
7. _____ secondary complaints
8. _____ exacerbate
9. _____ symptoms
10. _____ acute
11. _____ chronic
12. _____ differential diagnosis

a. the patient's primary problem or complaint
b. the information on the chart provided by the patient
c. the complete list of possible causes of the symptoms
d. a systematic approach consisting of hypotheses, observation, measurement, testing, and forming a conclusion
e. all other patient complaints after the main complaint or problem
f. an injury or condition having first occurred within the last few days or weeks
g. things an examiner observes during the examination, such as edema or erythema
h. sign or changes in health status that could indicate illness or injury
i. human creative skills the practitioner brings to the treatment of illness and injury
j. to make the symptoms worse and more pronounced
k. the actual cause of the symptoms or change in health status
l. a condition or set of symptoms present for an extended period of time

Investigation 2.0/2.1 Dr. _____

Medical Examination/Chief Complaint P._____ Date_____

Vocabulary 3: Sentences

Directions: Use each term below in a complete sentence.

1. subjective findings: _____
   _____

2. objective findings: _____
   _____

3. diagnosis: _____
   _____

4. scientific method: _____
   _____

5. art of medicine: _____
   _____

6. chief complaint: _____
   _____

7. secondary complaints: _____
   _____

8. exacerbate: _____
   _____

9. symptoms: _____
   _____

10. acute: _____
    _____

11. chronic: _____
    _____

12. differential diagnosis: _____
    _____

Investigation 2.0   Dr._____

Worksheet 2.0   P.____Date:_____

The Medical Diagnostic Process

1. How did medical practice probably begin thousands of years ago at the very beginning of man's evolution?

2. What does 'subjective' information refer to?

3. How is 'objective' information different from 'subjective' information?

4. What is a 'diagnosis'?

5. What does the word 'critical' mean when describing the condition of a patient?

6. Describe the 'Scientific Method' as utilized in the practice of medicine.

7. Describe how physicians use both **art** and **science** in treating patients.

Investigation 2.1   Dr._____

Activity 2.1   P.___ Date:_____

Activity 2.1:

Think about the last time you went to the doctor. Did the nurse or doctor ask you questions like the ones above? Answer the questions above for that occasion (or make up a new problem) on a piece of paper. Now team up with a fellow student. Decide who will be the doctor and who will be the patient. The doctor will attempt to determine the patient's chief complaint details by asking questions. Then switch roles. Remember, medical investigation involves asking lots of questions. Ask each other these questions, and more if you think of additional questions related to their medical history or complaint.

- What makes it feel better?
- What makes you feel worse?
- Is the problem always in the same place or does it move around?
- What have you tried already before coming here?
- Is the problem constant or does it come and go?
- Is the problem getting better, worse, or staying the same?
- What activities **exacerbate** the problem?
- Does anyone else in your family have this problem?

Interview notes: (write down things you learn about your patient)

_____

_____

_____

_____

_____

_____

_____

_____

_____

_____

Investigation 2.2　　　　　　　　　　　　　　　　　　　　Dr. _____

Medical History　　　　　　　　　　　　　　　　　　　P._____Date_____

Vocabulary 1: Definitions

Directions: Use the text, a dictionary, or the internet. Write a definition for each term below.

1. chief complaint: _____
   _____

2. medical history: _____
   _____

3. gender: _____
   _____

4. lifestyle: _____
   _____

5. genetic: _____
   _____

6. medicines: _____
   _____

7. overdose: _____
   _____

8. sub-acute: _____
   _____

9. side effects: _____
   _____

10. surgery: _____
    _____

11. art: _____
    _____

12. judgement: _____
    _____

Investigation 2.2

Medical History

Vocabulary 2: Matching

Dr. _____

P._____Date_____

Directions: Match the description on the right to the medical term on the left.

1. _____ chief complaint
2. _____ medical history
3. _____ gender
4. _____ lifestyle
5. _____ genetic
6. _____ medicines
7. _____ overdose
8. _____ sub-acute
9. _____ side effects
10. _____ surgery
11. _____ art of medicine
12. _____ judgement

a. traits or diseases inherited from your parents
b. the patient's primary problem
c. unintended effects or symptoms caused by a treatment
d. drugs prescribed to treat medical problems
e. male or female
f. the ability to make the right decision
g. the part of medical practice that goes beyond the science
h. the past medical problems as related by the patient
i. taking too much of a medicine
j. the habits that influence our lives
k. an illness or injury that remains symptomatic after several weeks
l. an invasive procedure to locate or correct an anatomical problem

Investigation 2.2 Dr. _____

Medical History P._____ Date_____

Vocabulary 3: Sentences

Directions: Use each medical term below in a complete sentence.

1. chief complaint: _____
   _____

2. medical history: _____
   _____

3. gender: _____
   _____

4. lifestyle: _____
   _____

5. genetic: _____
   _____

6. medicines: _____
   _____

7. overdose: _____
   _____

8. sub-acute: _____
   _____

9. side effects: _____
   _____

10. surgery: _____
    _____

11. art of medicine: _____
    _____

12. judgement: _____
    _____

Activity 2.2.1: Noting important details in the medical history

It is important to make note of any positive medical history findings. Any positive findings in the medical history questionnaire should be confirmed with the patient. For example, "In the medical history you wrote that you have had diabetes for 5 years; is this correct?"

Using the information provided for Patients 1 and 2 on the following pages, circle boldly or highlight all positive factors in the patient's medical history. After you have identified all of the positives, role play with a partner. Take turns being the doctor. Interview your patient about the positives in their medical history. Ask questions about the positives to get more information.

Patient 1
Medical History

Patient Name: use your name or a pseudo-name of your choice

Age: 61 **Birthdate:** your birthdate   **Gender:**   Female

Occupation: outside sales

Chief Complaint: headaches and occasional palpitations in chest

Current Medicines: aspirin for headaches, Maalox for stomach upset, estrogen

Past Medical Conditions: stomach ulcer treated 10 years ago

Last medical Evaluation: 5 years ago

Childhood Illnesses: strep throat, pink eye, roseola

Past Medical History

1. Stomach ulcer treated 10 yrs ago
2. 2 children by C-section many years ago

Family Medical History

Mother: uterine cancer

Father: hypertension and heart condition

Siblings: older brother has heart condition and hypertension

Surgical History

Cataract left eye 2 years ago

C- Section 39 and 41 years ago

Hysterectomy age 54

Activity 2.2.1   **Patient 2**

Medical History

Patient Name: use your name or a pseudo-name of your choice

Age: 43 **Birthdate:** your birthday   **Gender:** Male

Occupation: jack hammer operator

Chief Complaint: numbness and tingling in fingers and hands, weakness in hands and arms

Current Medicines:

1. Aspirin 325 mg as needed for headaches and hand pain

2. Advair steroid inhaler

Past Medical Conditions:

1. asthma since childhood

Last Medical Evaluation: 8 years ago

Childhood Illnesses:

1. Chicken pox
2. Measles
3. Mumps

Past Medical History

1. Asthma since childhood
2. Allergies to cat dander, grasses and pollens
3. Broken left wrist 11 years ago

Family Medical History

Mother: type 2 diabetes

Father: heart condition

Siblings: sister has type 1 diabetes

Surgical History

Tonsillectomy age 4

Appendectomy age 14

Wisdom teeth removed (4) age 23

Investigation 2.3/2.4   Dr. _____

Review of System/Exam   P._____ Date_____

Vocabulary 1: Definitions

Directions: Use the text, a dictionary, or the internet to write a definition for each term.

1. review of systems: _____
   _____

2. positives: _____
   _____

3. negatives: _____
   _____

4. differential diagnosis: _____
   _____

5. chart: _____
   _____

6. follow-up: _____
   _____

7. contiguous: _____
   _____

8. auscultation: _____
   _____

9. paresthesia: _____
   _____

10. stethoscope: _____
    _____

11. tissue: _____
    _____

12. ultrasound: _____
    _____

Investigation 2.3/2.4　　　　　　　　　　　　　　　　Dr. _____

Review of System/Exam　　　　　　　　　　　　　　P._____Date_____

Vocabulary 2: Matching

Directions: Match the definitions at the right to the medical term at the left.

1. _____ review of systems
2. _____ positives
3. _____ negatives
4. _____ differential diagnosis
5. _____ chart
6. _____ follow-up
7. _____ contiguous
8. _____ auscultation
9. _____ paresthesia
10. _____ stethoscope
11. _____ tissue
12. _____ ultrasound

a. abnormal perception of tingling or prickling in peripheral nerves
b. cells and their products making up the various materials in your body
c. the list of all possible causes of the symptoms under investigation
d. the organs of an area of the body that touch one another
e. part of the history taking where the physician asks the patient about each and every organ system to avoid missing any symptoms
f. the use of sound waves to visualize soft tissue structures
g. abnormal findings noted in the medical history or examination
h. the patient record of past and current medical information
i. the most often used medical instrument carried by most physicians about their neck
j. when the patient returns for re-evaluation of a problem
k. information or symptoms not experienced by the patient or not found by the physician during the examination
l. listening to the sounds of the heart, lungs, and other organs, usually using a stethoscope

Investigation 2.3/2.4 Dr. _____

Review of Systems/Exam P._____ Date_____

Vocabulary 3: Sentences

Directions: Use each term below in a complete sentence.

1. review of systems: _____
   _____

2. positives: _____
   _____

3. negatives: _____
   _____

4. differential diagnosis: _____
   _____

5. chart: _____
   _____

6. follow-up: _____
   _____

7. contiguous: _____
   _____

8. auscultation: _____
   _____

9. paresthesia: _____
   _____

10. stethoscope: _____
    _____

11. tissue: _____
    _____

12. ultrasound: _____
    _____

Activity 2.3A: Charting Positives from the Medical History in Review of Systems (ROS)

Using the section titled **ROS** (doctors rarely write "Review of Systems"; doctors often abbreviate it ROS), use the sample medical history chart on the following pages to write in the <u>positive</u> past medical history (**Hx**) information you want available for review for patients one and two.

Patient 1: Medical History

Patient Name: use your name or a pseudo-name of your choice

Age: 43 **Birthdate:** your birthday   **Gender:** Male

Occupation: jack hammer operator

Chief Complaint: numbness and tingling in fingers and hands, weakness in hands and arms

Current Medicines:

1. aspirin 325 mg as needed for headaches and hand pain

2. Advair steroid inhaler

Past Medical Conditions:

1. asthma since childhood

Last Medical Evaluation: 8 years ago

Childhood Illnesses:

1. Chicken pox
2. Measles
3. Mumps

Past Medical History

1. Asthma since childhood
2. Allergies to cat dander, grasses and pollens
3. Broken left wrist 11 years ago

Family Medical History

Mother: type 2 diabetes, Alzheimers

Father: heart condition, prostate cancer

Siblings: sister has type 1 diabetes

Surgical History

Tonsillectomy age 4

Appendectomy age 14

Wisdom teeth removed (4) age 23

- **Use the space on the following page to make notes regarding your review of systems from patient #1. Write positive findings from history**

Investigation 2.3 Dr._____

Activity 2.3A P.____Date:_____

Patient 1

Review of Systems

Patient Name: _____ Age:_____ Gender: M F

ROS:

Mental Status:
_____

Cardiac (heart):
_____

Circulatory: _____

Respiratory (lungs):_____

Digestive: _____

Urinary:
_____

Reproductive:
_____

Dermatologic:
_____

Extremities: _____

Areas of concern or requiring additional information:

_____

_____

_____

_____

_____

Investigation 2.3

Activity 2.3B

Patient 2:
Medical History

Patient Name: use your name or a pseudo-name of your choice

Age: 61 **Birthdate:** your birthdate   **Gender:**   Female

Occupation: outside sales

Chief Complaint: headaches and occasional palpitations in chest

Current Medicines: aspirin for headaches, Maalox for stomach upset, estrogen

Past Medical Conditions: stomach ulcer treated 10 years ago

Last medical Evaluation: 5 years ago

Childhood Illnesses: strep throat, pink eye, roseola

Past Medical History

3. Stomach ulcer treated 10 yrs ago
4. 2 children by C-section many years ago

Family Medical History

Mother: uterine cancer

Father: hypertension and heart condition

Siblings: older brother has heart condition and hypertension

Surgical History

Cataract left eye 2 years ago

C- Section 39 and 41 years ago

Hysterectomy age 54

Investigation 2.3   Dr._____

Activity 2.3.B   P.____Date:_____

Patient 2

Review of Systems

Patient Name: _____Age:_____ Gender: M F

ROS:

Mental Status:
_____

Cardiac (heart):
_____

Circulatory: _____

Respiratory (lungs):_____

Digestive: _____

Urinary: _____

Reproductive:
_____

Dermatologic:
_____

Extremities: _____

Areas of concern or requiring additional information:

_____

_____

_____

_____

_____

Investigation 2.4 – Medical Exam   Dr._____

Activity 2.4: Body Systems   P.____Date:_____

Directions: Match the body system that are part of your examination on the left with members of each system on the right.

1. Cardiovascular System
2. Digestive System, Primary
3. Digestive System, Secondary
4. Endocrine System
5. Integumentary System
6. Lymphatic System
7. Muscular System
8. Nervous System
9. Reproductive System, Male
10. Reproductive System, Female
11. Respiratory System
12. Skeletal System
13. Urinary System

_____ Nose, Pharynx, Larynx, Trachea, Bronchi, Lungs

_____ Brain, Spinal cord, Nerves

_____ Kidneys, Ureters, Urinary bladder, Urethra

_____ Pituitary gland, Pineal gland, Hypothalamus, Thyroid gland, Parathyroid

_____ Teeth, Salivary glands, Tongue, Liver, Gallbladder, Pancreas

_____ Lymph nodes, Lymph vessels, Thymus, Spleen, Tonsils

_____ Heart, Blood vessels

_____ Skin, Hair, Nails, Sense receptors, Sweat gland, Oil glands

_____ Mouth, Pharynx, Esophagus, Stomach, Small intestine, Large intestine, Rectum

_____ Ovaries, Uterus, Fallopian Tubes, Mammary glands

_____ Bones, Joints

_____ Muscles

_____ Testes, vas Deferens, Urethra, Prostate

Investigation 2.4

Activity 2.4

Activity 1: Testing the Plantar Response. Find a partner. Take off your shoes and socks. Have your partner sit on a table or desk with their feet hanging in a relaxed manner. Using a neurological hammer if you have one, or the eraser end of a pencil, rub the eraser along the outside surface of the bottom of your partner's feet, one foot, then the other foot. You should observe the big toe move downward without any effort from your partner.

When you get home you can check your brothers and sisters plantar reflexes by using the eraser end of a pencil. If you check your baby brother or sister you need to know that it is normal for very young children to have a positive test, or upward movement of the big toe. In older children and adults the big toe should move downward.

Investigation 2.5/2.6　　　　　　　　　　　　　　　　　　　Dr. _____

Differential Diagnosis/Diagnosis　　　　　　　　　　P._____Date_____

Vocabulary 1: Definitions

Directions: Use the text, a dictionary, or the internet to write a definition for each term.

1. differential diagnosis: _____
   _____

2. priority: _____
   _____

3. rule out: _____
   _____

4. pulmonary: _____
   _____

5. cardiac: _____
   _____

6. musculoskeletal: _____
   _____

7. diagnosis: _____
   _____

8. symptoms: _____
   _____

9. infection: _____
   _____

10. injury: _____
    _____

11. genetic disorder: _____
    _____

12. communicable: _____
    _____

Investigation 2.5/2.6 Dr. _____

Differential Diagnosis/Diagnosis P._____ Date _____

Vocabulary 2: Matching

Directions: Match the definitions at the right to the medical terms on the left.

1. _____ differential diagnosis
2. _____ priority
3. _____ rule out
4. _____ pulmonary
5. _____ cardiac
6. _____ musculoskeletal
7. _____ diagnosis
8. _____ symptoms
9. _____ infection
10. _____ injury
11. _____ genetic disorder
12. _____ communicable

a. the body system consisting of bones, muscles, and joints
b. the list of possible causes of a set of symptoms
c. a disease capable of spreading to others
d. related to the respiratory system
e. what you get when invaded by pathogenic germs
f. your most important focus or interest
g. changes in health status that may provide clues about the cause
h. a disease passed on by parents to their children at birth
i. pertaining to the heart
j. what you have when you sprain your ankle
k. the process by which you remove an item from the differential diagnosis
l. the cause of the symptoms investigated

Investigation 2.5/2.6

Differential Diagnosis/Diagnosis

Vocabulary 3: Sentences

Dr. _____

P. _____ Date _____

Directions: Use each term below in a complete sentence.

1. differential diagnosis: _____
   _____

2. priority: _____
   _____

3. rule out: _____
   _____

4. pulmonary: _____
   _____

5. cardiac: _____
   _____

6. musculoskeletal: _____
   _____

7. diagnosis: _____
   _____

8. symptoms: _____
   _____

9. infection: _____
   _____

10. injury: _____
    _____

11. genetic disorder: _____
    _____

12. communicable: _____
    _____

Investigation 2.5   Dr._____

Activity 2.5.4   P.____ Date:_____

Differential Diagnosis for Headaches

Headaches are another disorder having many potential causes. Suppose your patient complains of headaches and wants you to investigate what is causing them. You don't want to let your patient down. Make a Differential Diagnosis for headaches. Think of as many things that could cause a headache to occur. Then think about which are the most serious potential causes and place an 'S' (for serious) next to them. These would be the conditions or causes you would want to rule out first.

Headache Differential Diagnosis (DDx):

(Hint: According to the Mayo Clinic [2], there are seven primary causes of headaches and over twenty-five secondary causes of headaches) How many can you think of?

1. _____
2. _____
3. _____
4. _____
5. _____
6. _____
7. _____
8. _____
9. _____
10. _____ 10 = you're a star
11. _____
12. _____
13. _____
14. _____
15. _____ 15 = you're a Super Star
16. _____
17. _____
18. _____
19. _____
20. _____ 20 = Are you in med school?

Ref: http://www.mayoclinic.org/symptoms/headache/basics/causes/sym-20050800

Investigation 2.6 Dr._____

Worksheet 2.6.5 P.____Date:_____

Diagnosis: Infection, Injury, or Genetic Cause

One of the initial challenges you have as a physician is to classify your patient's chief complaint. In this activity you will practice classifying disorders into their category.

Legend: Caused by Infection = **INF**   Caused by Injury = **INJ**   Genetic cause = **GEN**

_____ Natural Red Hair

_____ Sprained Ankle after soccer game

_____ Stomach ache after eating potato salad at picnic

_____ Pimples on face

_____ Concussion after football game

_____ Down Syndrome

_____ Chicken Pox

_____ Infected ingrown toenail

_____ Cystic Fibrosis

_____ Blue Eyes

_____ Fractured wrist after a fall

_____ Muscular Dystrophy

_____ Fractured Pelvis after a car accident

_____ Polio

_____ Infant born with six toes on each foot

_____ Ebola

_____ Quadriplegic after fall from roof

_____ Small Pox

_____ 2nd degree burns after a fire

_____ Tuberculosis   # Correct: _____ /20

Investigation 2.7

Dr. _____

SOAP Notes

P._____Date_____

Vocabulary 1: Definitions

Directions: Use the text, a dictionary, or the internet to write a definition for each term.

1. SOAP: _____

2. subjective: _____

3. objective: _____

4. assessment: _____

5. plan: _____

6. edema: _____

7. extension: _____

8. flexion: _____

9. prescription: _____

10. sickness: _____

11. injury: _____

12. organization: _____

Investigation 2.7

SOAP Notes

Vocabulary 2: Matching

Dr. _____

P._____Date_____

Directions: Match the definitions at the right to the medical terms on the left.

1. _____ SOAP
2. _____ subjective findings
3. _____ objective findings
4. _____ assessment
5. _____ diagnostic plan
6. _____ edema
7. _____ extension
8. _____ flexion
9. _____ prescription
10. _____ sickness
11. _____ injury
12. _____ organization

a. follow-up notes using Subjective, Objective, Assessment, Plan
b. straightening of a joint, such as your elbow
c. an example is a deep cut on your arm resulting from a bike accident
d. tests you will perform to find the cause of your patient's symptoms
e. a key to success in school and a successful medical practice
f. what patients probably have when they visit their physician for a sore throat and cough
g. bending your knee
h. things you observe during your examination of a patient
i. a cause of soft tissue swelling
j. how your patient has been feeling
k. what you write to the pharmacist so your patient can get their medicine
l. your opinion or diagnosis as written in your soap notes

Investigation 2.7

SOAP Notes

Vocabulary 3: Sentences

Dr. _____

P._____ Date_____

Directions: Use each term below in a complete sentence.

1. SOAP: _____
   _____

2. subjective: _____
   _____

3. objective: _____
   _____

4. assessment: _____
   _____

5. plan: _____
   _____

6. edema: _____
   _____

7. extension: _____
   _____

8. flexion: _____
   _____

9. prescription: _____
   _____

10. sickness: _____
    _____

11. injury: _____
    _____

12. organization: _____
    _____

Investigation 2.7 Dr._____

Activity 2.7.4 P.____ Date:_____

SOAP Note Activity 1

1. What does the S in SOAP stand for? _____

2. Write a definition of "Subjective Findings".

   _____
   _____

3. Give two examples of "Subjective Findings" from a hypothetical patient visit.

   a. _____

   b. _____

4. What does the 'O' in SOAP stand for? _____

5. Write a definition of "Objective Findings"

   _____
   _____

6. Give two examples of "Objective Findings" from a hypothetical patient visit.

   a. _____

   b. _____

7. What does the A in SOAP stand for? _____

8. Write a definition of "Assessment" from your hypothetical patient visit notes.

   _____
   _____

Investigation 2.7 Dr._____
Activity 2.7.4, page 2

9. Provide two examples of possible "Assessment" entries in your patient notes.

    a. _____

    b. _____

10. What does the "P" in SOAP stand for? _____

11. Write a definition of "Plan" as it pertain to your patient notes.

    _____

    _____

12. Provide two examples of things you might write in your Plan for your hypothetical patient.

    a. _____

    b. _____

13. What is the name of the physician who in 1968 first described the concept of "SOAP Notes"? _____

14. What problem was Dr. Weed attempting to solve by the introduction of "SOAP Notes"?

    _____

    _____

    _____

Investigation 2.7

Activity 2.7.5

Dr._____

P.____Date:_____

SOAP Note Activity 2

Directions: Make up a hypothetical patient of your own. Think of at least five entries for Subjective and Objective findings. You should have at least three entries in the Assessment and Plan sections. Write out a set of SOAP notes on that patient.

Investigation 2.0 – 2.7   Dr._____

Crossword 2.7.6   **Medical Diagnosis**   P.____Date:_____

Directions: Use the highlighted terms in chapters 2.1 through 2.7 to solve the puzzle. Most clues come from the text, but some may require outside investigation. Omit spaces or dashes between words.

Medical Investigation 101 - Hill & Griffith

ACROSS

2 an instrument used to measure blood pressure
4 acronym for magnetic resonance imaging
8 the next visit for the same medical problem
10 the reason someone has red hair, or a long life line on their hand, or brown eyes
12 'yes' answers on the review of systems; things not to be forgotten about the patient
15 the part of the practice of medicine that relies on experience, judgment, and intuition to make the diagnosis
17 abnormal sensory perception to physical or electrical stimuli
21 listening to the sounds of the heart, lungs, or abdomen
22 conditions or symptoms present for an extended period of time
25 information based on feelings and opinions, rather than direct observation or measurement
26 information gained from touching, measuring, or observing
27 male or female
28 identifying the cause of the symptoms, illness, or injury
29 unintended effects caused by treatment or medicines
30 conditions or symptoms of recent onset
31 the areas adjacent to the patient's pain or examination area

DOWN

1 illnesses that can be easily spread to others
3 a list of the possible causes for a set of symtoms or a condition
5 the patient's main problem or area of concern
6 a positive plantar reflex where the big toes moves upward to stimulation along the outside bottom of the foot
7 the condition where a patient is extremely sick or near death
9 sound wave test used to see a developing fetus
11 standardized method of notetaking at followup patient visits
13 important clues about how a patient is feeling
14 taking too much of a drug or medicine
16 things animals other than humans do to medicate themselves
18 important tool of a physician; used to listen to the heart and lungs
19 to make the condition or symptoms worse
20 medical shorthand for 'review of systems'
23 the portion of the practice of medicine based on known information and proven evaluation tools
24 the 'no' answers on the system review; things that do not apply to that patient

Investigation 3.1A   Dr._____

Breathing Difficulty   P._____Date_____

Vocabulary 1: Definitions

Directions: Use the text, a dictionary, or the internet to write a definition for each term.

1. agitated: _____
   _____

2. contract (as in "contract a disease"):_____
   _____

3. sprain: _____
   _____

4. stethoscope: _____
   _____

5. breath sounds: _____
   _____

6. oximeter: _____
   _____

7. oxygen saturation: _____
   _____

8. pneumonia: _____
   _____

9. tuberculosis:_____
   _____

10. hiatal hernia:_____
    _____

11. pulmonary embolus: _____
    _____

12. obese: _____
    _____

Investigation 3.1A Dr. _____

Breathing Difficulty P._____Date_____

Vocabulary 2: Matching

Directions: Match each definition on the right to the medical term on the left.

1. _____ agitated
2. _____ contract
3. _____ sprain
4. _____ stethoscope
5. _____ breath sounds
6. _____ oximeter
7. _____ oxygen saturation
8. _____ pneumonia
9. _____ tuberculosis
10. _____ hiatal hernia
11. _____ pulmonary embolus
12. _____ obese

a. primary physician tool for hearing heart, breath, and bowel sounds
b. to become infected with an infectious disease
c. lung inflammation caused by bacterial or viral infection
d. severely overweight
e. instrument for measuring the proportion of oxygenated hemoglobin in blood
f. protrusion of the stomach through the esophageal opening in the diaphragm
g. an infectious bacterial disease having growth of nodules in the lungs
h. feeling or appearing nervous or troubled
i. the percentage of oxygen-saturated hemoglobin compared to total blood hemoglobin
j. an injury characterized by damage to one or more ligaments
k. a sudden blockage of an artery in the lung, usually caused by a clot moving from a leg vein
l. sounds of air moving through lungs during inspiration and exhalation, and heard through a stethoscope

Investigation 3.1A Dr. _____

Breathing Difficulty P._____ Date_____

Vocabulary 3: Sentences

Directions: Use each term in a sentence.

1. agitated: _____
   _____

2. contract: _____
   _____

3. sprain: _____
   _____

4. stethoscope: _____
   _____

5. breath sounds: _____
   _____

6. oximeter: _____
   _____

7. oxygen saturation: _____
   _____

8. pneumonia: _____
   _____

9. tuberculosis: _____
   _____

10. hiatal hernia: _____
    _____

11. pulmonary embolus: _____
    _____

12. obese: _____
    _____

Investigation 3.1A Dr._____

Breathing Difficulty P.____Date:_____

Worksheet 3.1.4

Breathing Difficulty Case 1 Worksheet

Directions: Answer the following questions based on Case 3.1: Breathing Difficulty.

1. What is the patient's Chief Complaint? _____
2. What was the patient's Secondary Complaint? _____
3. How many breaths per minute were detected in the examination? _____/min
4. What is the normal rate of breathing for a patient her age: _____/min
5. Using a watch with a second hand, count the number of breaths you take in a minute and record here: _____ breaths/minute
6. What does an "oximeter" measure? _____
7. What was the result of the oximeter test done on Betsy at the end of the examination? _____%
8. What is the "normal" finding on the oximeter test? _____%
9. What does Betsy's oximeter test result indicate?

    _____

10. Do you think Betsy's ankle sprain could have caused Betsy's breathing difficulty?

    Circle: Yes   No

11. Would you classify Betsy's condition as (circle one)   Acute or Chronic

12. Would you classify Betsy's condition as (circle one):

    Possible Emergency or Probable Non-Emergency

Investigation 3.1A

Worksheet 3.1.4, page 2

Dr._____

13. From the chart below select the <u>top three</u> on your Differential Diagnosis List of things you want to <u>rule out</u> on this patient.

Differential Diagnosis	Yes	No
Pneumonia		
Anxiety Reaction		
Pulmonary Embolus		
Asthma		
Pulmonary Hypertension		
Heart Failure		
Chronic Obstructive Pulmonary Disease		
Tuberculosis		

14. Do you think Betsy should be sent to a specialist for more evaluation or would you feel comfortable sending her home to rest for a few days before returning for further evaluation if the breathing difficulty continues?

    (Circle one)   Send to Specialist   or   Send Home to rest

15. If you sent Betsy to a specialist, to which one would you send her?

Investigation 3.1B   Dr. _____

Pulmonary Embolism   P._____ Date_____

Vocabulary 1: Definitions

Directions: Use the text, a dictionary, or the internet to write a definition for each term.

1. pulmonary: _____
   _____

2. embolism: _____
   _____

3. blood clot: _____
   _____

4. thrombolytic: _____
   _____

5. central circulation: _____
   _____

6. anticoagulant: _____
   _____

7. emboli: _____
   _____

8. air exchange: _____
   _____

9. obstruction: _____
   _____

Investigation 3.1B　　　　　　　　　　　　　　　　　　Dr. _____

Pulmonary Embolism　　　　　　　　　　　　　　　　P._____ Date_____

Vocabulary 2: Matching

Directions: Match the definitions at the right to the medical terms on the left.

1. _____ pulmonary
2. _____ embolism
3. _____ blood clot
4. _____ thrombolytic
5. _____ central circulation
6. _____ anticoagulant
7. _____ emboli
8. _____ air exchange
9. _____ obstruction

a. a mass of semi-coagulated blood that can travel through veins and become lodged in an artery
b. movement of blood through the arteries and veins of the body, caused by the pumping of the heart
c. The transference of oxygen and carbon dioxide in the alveoli of the lungs
d. Referring to the respiratory tract
e. a blockage of the flow of air or blood, or movement of food in the intestinal tract
f. a type of medicine having the ability to break apart blood clots
g. a type of medicine having the ability to slow or block the blood clotting process
h. blockage of an artery by a blood clot, fatty deposit, or air bubble
i. plural form of embolus

Investigation 3.1B

Pulmonary Embolism

Vocabulary 3: Sentences

Dr. _____

P. _____ Date _____

Directions: Write a sentence using each term.

1. pulmonary: _____
   _____

2. embolism: _____
   _____

3. blood clot: _____
   _____

4. thrombolytic: _____
   _____

5. central circulation: _____
   _____

6. anticoagulant: _____
   _____

7. emboli: _____
   _____

8. air exchange: _____
   _____

9. obstruction: _____
   _____

Investigation 3.1B Dr._____

Worksheet 3.1B.4 P___ Date:_____

Pulmonary Embolism

Directions: Answer the following questions.

1. What does the term "Pulmonary" refer to? _____

2. What is an "Embolism"? _____

3. What is an "Embolus"? _____

4. Is a pulmonary embolism an acute or chronic problem? Explain your answer.

   _____
   _____
   _____
   _____

5. What is the most likely cause of Betsy's pulmonary embolism?

   _____

6. Explain how a pulmonary embolism causes difficulty breathing?

   _____
   _____
   _____
   _____

7. What is a 'thrombolytic drug"? _____

   _____

8. Why is it important to begin thrombolytic drug therapy as soon as possible?

   _____
   _____

Investigation 3.1A/B   Dr._____

Crossword 3.1.5A/B: Pulmonary Embolism   P.____Date:_____

Directions: Use the highlighted terms in the chapter to solve the puzzle. Most clues come from the chapter text, but some require outside investigation. Omit spaces or dashes between words.

Medical Investigation 101 - Hill & Griffith

ACROSS

1. a tool of physicians used to listen to heart, lung, and bowel sounds
6. the trading places of oygen and carbon dioxide in the alveoli of the lungs
8. of very recent onset
9. an obstruction of a blood vessel by air bubble, fat, or blood clot
10. a drug designed to break up a blood clot
11. an injury where ligaments are stretched or ruptured
13. the blood moving through the heart and lungs
14. a list of possible causes of a set of symptoms
15. when most muscles shorten and exert their power

DOWN

2. having the ability to stretch
3. a condition that lasts a long time
4. means lung; the system containing the trachea, bronchi, bronchioles, and alveoli
5. thepercent of oxygen carrying capability of blood; compromised in respiratory diseases
6. a medicine designed to slow or prevent blood clotting
7. a device placed on the finger that measures the percent oxygen saturation of blood; under 90% is considered low
12. feeling or appearing troubled or nervous

Investigation 3.2A

Dr. _____

Abdominal Pain

P._____ Date_____

Vocabulary 1: Definitions

Directions: Use the text, a dictionary, or the internet to write a definition for each term.

1. abdominal cavity: _____
   _____

2. quadrant: _____
   _____

3. umbilicus: _____
   _____

4. gurney: _____
   _____

5. subtle: _____
   _____

6. pancreatitis: _____
   _____

7. cholangitis: _____
   _____

8. gastric: _____
   _____

9. hepatoma: _____
   _____

10. appendicitis: _____
    _____

11. metastasis: _____
    _____

12. purulence: _____
    _____

Investigation 3.2A

Abdominal Pain

Dr. _____

P._____ Date_____

Vocabulary 2: Matching

Directions: Match each definition on the right with the medical term on the left.

1. _____ abdominal cavity
2. _____ quadrant
3. _____ umbilicus
4. _____ gurney
5. _____ subtle
6. _____ pancreatitis
7. _____ cholangitis
8. _____ gastric
9. _____ hepatoma
10. _____ appendicitis
11. _____ metastasis
12. _____ purulence

a. The space containing your lower esophagus, stomach, small intestine, colon, rectum, liver, gallbladder, pancreas, spleen, kidneys, and bladder

b. cancer originating in the liver

c. a wheeled stretcher used to transport patients

d. inflammation and pain related to the appendix

e. a secondary growth occurring away from the original site of cancer

f. a bacterial infection of the bile duct

g. division of the abdominal area into four areas placing the umbilicus in the center

h. synonym for pus

i. referring to the stomach

j. your navel or belly button

k. very delicate or highly precise

l. inflammation of the pancreas

Investigation 3.2A

Abdominal Pain

Vocabulary 3: Sentences

Dr. _____

P._____ Date_____

Directions: Write a sentence using each term.

1. abdominal cavity: _____
   _____

2. quadrant: _____
   _____

3. umbilicus: _____
   _____

4. gurney: _____
   _____

5. subtle: _____
   _____

6. pancreatitis: _____
   _____

7. cholangitis: _____
   _____

8. gastric: _____
   _____

9. hepatoma: _____
   _____

10. appendicitis: _____
    _____

11. metastasis: _____
    _____

12. purulence: _____
    _____

Investigation 3.2A Dr. _____

Worksheet 3.2A1 P.____ Date:_____

Abdominal Pain Worksheet

1. Name the four quadrants of the abdomen.

    a. _____

    b. _____

    c. _____

    d. _____

2. Which organs are located in the right upper quadrant?

    a. _____

    b. _____

    c. _____

    d. _____

    e. _____

3. Which organs are found in the left upper quadrant?

    a. _____

    b. _____

    c. _____

    d. _____

    e. _____

4. What would you expect to find in the right lower quadrant?

    a. _____

    b. _____

    c. _____

    d. _____

    e. _____

Investigation 3.2A - Abdominal Pain   Dr._____

Worksheet 3.2A1

Page 2

5. Which organs reside in the left lower quadrant?

   a. _____
   b. _____
   c. _____
   d. _____

6. List the six clues given by Crystal's Mother in the history?

   a. _____
   b. _____
   c. _____
   d. _____
   e. _____
   f. _____

7. Which six clues did you discover in your examination?

   a. _____
   b. _____
   c. _____
   d. _____
   e. _____
   f. _____

8. Which conditions did you immediately eliminate from your initial differential diagnosis list?

   a. _____
   b. _____
   c. _____
   d. _____
   e. _____

Investigation 3.2A – Abdominal Pain Dr. _____

Worksheet 3.2A1 P.____ Date:_____

Page 3

9. Which three conditions are the prime suspects in our investigation?

   a. _____

   b. _____

   c. _____

10. Which three medical tests did you elect to order at the beginning of your investigation?

    a. _____

    b. _____

    c. _____

11. What was your final diagnosis?

    _____

12. What was your first treatment recommendation?

    _____

13. What treatment would you recommend if your initial treatment proved unsuccessful in curing Crystal's illness?

    _____

14. Why was it important to treat this condition immediately and aggressively?

    _____

    _____

15. What are the primary risks inherent in any surgical procedure?

    a. _____

    b. _____

Investigation 3.2A Dr._____

Worksheet 3.2A1

Page 4

16. Identify the structures in each abdominal quadrant shown below.

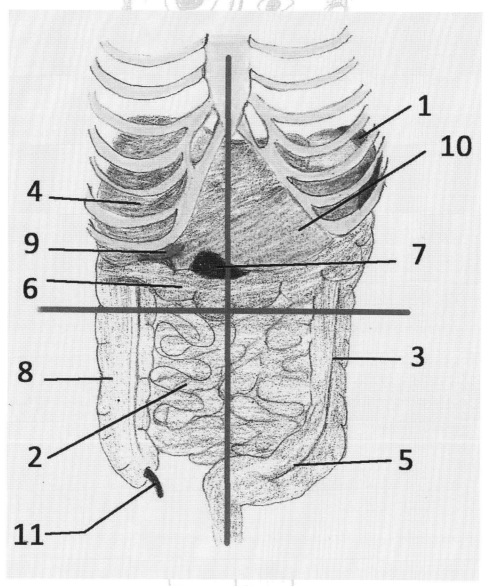

Directions: Write the name of the organ identified by each number in the diagram above.

1. _____
2. _____
3. _____
4. _____
5. _____
6. _____
7. _____
8. _____
9. _____
10. _____
11. _____

Investigation 3.2A Dr._____

Crossword 3.2A **Abdominal Pain** P.____ Date:_____

Directions: Use the highlighted terms in the chapter to solve the puzzle. Most clues come from the chapter text, some require outside investigation. Omit spaces or dashes between words.

Medical Investigation 101 - Hill & Griffith

ACROSS

5 area containing stomach and several other important organs
7 restriction of blood flow to tissue
10 lasting for weeks, months, or even longer
12 a flat stretcher on wheels used for transporting patients
14 the regular, rhythmic beating of the heart
18 near the appendix; often refers to an infection of or near the appendix
21 the outward expansion of the abdomen from the accumulation of gas or fluid; typically a symptom of disease or bodily dysfunction
22 a tubular support placed inside a blood vessel to relieve a blockage
23 a measurement of breathing rate
24 the place of attachment of the umbilical cord to an fetus; the place of separation of the umbilical cord in a child or adult
25 e white outer layer of the eyeball

DOWN

1 of very recent onset
2 refers to stomach
3 the part of the abdominal cavity containing the liver, right kidney, gall bladder, and part of the pancreas
4 refers to pain upon removing pressure applied to abdomen; a sign of potential appendicitis or peritinitis
6 wider, larger, or more open than normal
8 the part of the body containing the organs of food digestion
9 inflammation of the appendix
11 the normal noises made by the stomach and intestines as food moves during peristalsis
13 signs and feelings experienced by the patient that help guide the doctor to appropriate medical tests and a diagnosis
15 a measurement of heart rate
16 a ballooning of a blood vessel; represents a weakening of the vessel that could rupture
17 one section of the abdominal area when divided into four areas
18 inflammation of the pancreas
19 an infection of the bile duct; bile is important in digestion of fats
20 lying face upward

Investigation 3.2B

Dr. _____

P. _____ Date _____

Microbes 1

Vocabulary 1A: Definitions

Directions: Use the text, a dictionary, or the internet to write a definition for each term.

1. miasma: _____
   _____

2. microorganisms: _____
   _____

3. carrier: _____
   _____

4. immunity: _____
   _____

5. membrane: _____
   _____

6. pores: _____
   _____

7. virus: _____
   _____

8. rabies: _____
   _____

9. microbes: _____
   _____

10. bacteria: _____
    _____

11. nanometer: _____
    _____

12. antibiotic: _____
    _____

Investigation 3.2B

Microbes 1

Vocabulary 2A: Matching #1

Dr. _____

P. _____ Date _____

Directions: Match the definitions on the right to the medical terms on the left.

1. _____ miasma
2. _____ microorganisms
3. _____ carrier
4. _____ immunity
5. _____ membrane
6. _____ pores
7. _____ virus
8. _____ rabies
9. _____ microbes
10. _____ bacteria
11. _____ nanometer
12. _____ antibiotic

a. one-billionth of a meter
b. a person infected with an infectious disease agent, but who has no symptoms
c. highly unpleasant or unhealthy smelling air
d. an organism's ability to resist a disease or infection
e. organisms so small they can be seen only with a microscope
f. a medicine having the ability to kill or prevent reproduction of bacteria
g. small openings through which gases, liquids, or microorganisms can pass
h. a microorganism causing disease
i. a fatal and contagious viral disease afflicting mammals and spread in saliva
j. a thin, flexible material that acts as a boundary or lining
k. a 'non-living' infectious organism capable of multiplying only in a host's living cells and visible under an electron microscope
l. one-celled living organisms visible with a light microscope, some of which cause disease

Investigation 3.2B

Microbes 1

Dr. _____

P. _____ Date _____

Vocabulary 3A: Sentences

Directions: Write a sentence using each term.

1. miasma: _____
   _____

2. microorganisms: _____
   _____

3. carrier: _____
   _____

4. immunity: _____
   _____

5. membrane: _____
   _____

6. pores: _____
   _____

7. virus: _____
   _____

8. rabies: _____
   _____

9. microbes: _____
   _____

10. bacteria: _____
    _____

11. nanometer: _____
    _____

12. antibiotic: _____
    _____

Investigation 3.2B

Microbes 2

Dr. _____

P. _____ Date _____

Vocabulary 1B: Definitions #2

Directions: Use the text, a dictionary, or the internet to write a definition for each term.

1. super-infection: _____
   _____

2. communicable: _____
   _____

3. vaccine: _____
   _____

4. febrile: _____
   _____

5. pandemic: _____
   _____

6. preventive: _____
   _____

7. epidemiologist: _____
   _____

8. unilateral: _____
   _____

9. paralysis: _____
   _____

10. viable: _____
    _____

11. syndrome: _____
    _____

12. abscess: _____
    _____

Investigation 3.2B

Microbes 2

Vocabulary 2B: Matching #2

Dr. _____

P._____Date_____

Directions: Match the definitions on the right to the medical terms on the left.

1. _____ super-infection
2. _____ communicable
3. _____ vaccine
4. _____ febrile
5. _____ pandemic
6. _____ preventive
7. _____ epidemiologist
8. _____ unilateral
9. _____ paralysis
10. _____ viable
11. _____ syndrome
12. _____ abscess

a. a set of signs and symptoms that appear together and define a medical condition
b. visible or occurring on only the left or right side
c. a disease prevalent or spreading over an entire country or the world
d. capable of being shared or spread to others
e. the inability to move a part or an entire body
f. a second infection occurring on top of or following an original infection
g. a scientist who studies the spread and control of diseases
h. capable of surviving in a given environment
i. a swollen, inflamed area of tissue containing an area of pus
j. measures taken to prevent the onset or spread of diseases
k. having an elevated body temperature
l. stimulates the production of antibodies to prevent a disease

Investigation 3.2B Dr. _____

Microbes 2 P._____ Date_____

Vocabulary 3B: Sentences

Directions: Write a sentence using each term.

1. super-infection: _____
   _____

2. communicable: _____
   _____

3. vaccine: _____
   _____

4. febrile: _____
   _____

5. pandemic: _____
   _____

6. preventive: _____
   _____

7. epidemiologist: _____
   _____

8. unilateral: _____
   _____

9. paralysis: _____
   _____

10. viable: _____
    _____

11. syndrome: _____
    _____

12. abscess: _____
    _____

Investigation 3.2B Dr._____

Worksheet 3.2B P._____ Date:_____

Viruses & Bacteria Worksheet

Answer the following questions based on your reading of chapter 3.2B.

1. In what ways are bacteria and viruses different?

    a. _____
    b. _____
    c. _____
    d. _____

2. Give four similarities between bacteria and viruses:

    a. _____
    b. _____
    c. _____
    d. _____

3. Name four ways bacteria and viruses spread:

    a. _____
    b. _____
    c. _____
    d. _____

4. True or False: All bacteria are harmful to humans.
    _____

5. Where do viruses reside?
    _____

6. What do viruses require in order to survive?

    _____

3.2B Viruses & Bacteria Worksheet   Dr._____

Page 2

7. About what percent of bacteria cause infections?

   _____%

8. What was the first antibiotic used to fight bacterial infection?

   _____

9. Why is penicillin not very effective treating most infections today?

   _____

10. What problem is caused by the overuse of antibiotics?

    _____

11. What is the most effective method of preventing viral infection?

    _____

12. What are four impossible measures that would almost guarantee that you would not catch a viral or bacterial infection?

    a. _____
    b. _____
    c. _____
    d. _____

13. Name four serious viral infections spread by mosquitos.

    a. _____
    b. _____
    c. _____
    d. _____

3.2B Viruses & Bacteria Worksheet Dr._____ P___

Page 3

14. Which organism has probably killed more people than any other in the last 100 years?
    _____

15. Which two insects transmit many of the most virulent viruses?
    a. _____
    b. _____

16. Which animals most commonly carry the rabies virus?
    a. _____
    b. _____
    c. _____
    d. _____
    e. _____

17. What preventive treatments are given to those bitten or scratched by an animal suspected of possibly having rabies?
    a. _____
    b. _____

18. Why is it important NOT to breathe water into your nose when swimming in a public swimming pool or lake?
    _____
    _____
    _____

19. How does polio affect girls and boys differently?
    a. Girls: _____
    b. Boys: _____

Investigation 3.3B   Dr._____

Worksheet 3.3B, page 4

Viruses & Bacteria

20. Aside from organisms contaminating drinking water, what else can end up in water that can cause illness?

    _____

21. Name two bacteria that can cause food poisoning.

    a. _____

    b. _____

22. What are three bacteria that can infect humans when breathed in?

    a. _____

    b. _____

    c. _____

23. How long have bacterial and viruses existed on Earth?

    _____

Investigation 3.2B Dr._____

Crossword 3.2B **Microbes** P.____ Date:_____

Directions: Use the highlighted terms in the chapter to solve the puzzle. Most clues come from the chapter text, some require outside investigation. Omit spaces or dashes between words.

discovered in Lyme, Connecticut
39 a set of symptoms that consistently occur together
40 things we do to prevent an illness or accident from occurring
41 the first Scientist to understand the real origin of infectious disease

DOWN

1 Invented a microscope; first one to actually see microbes
2 another name for a microorganism causing fermentation or disease
3 childhood viral disease; can cause shingles in adults who had chicken pox as a child
4 small holes or openings in a membrane, such as skin
7 a living microscopic organism present in the human body; about 1% of them cause disease
8 a high-powered microscope that uses electron beams instead of light
10 affecting either the left or right side of the body, but not both sides
14 a viral disease spread by mosquitos; causes microcephaly in babies born to infected mothers
15 capable of surviving in a particular environment
17 a disease capable of transmission from one sufferer to another
21 Italian scholar who decided about 1546 that 'miasma' did not make sense as the cause of sickness
22 an infectious viral disease affecting the central nervous system; causes scoliosis in girls and unilateral leg wasting in boys
24 a non-living microbe that attacks the RNA or DNA of host cells
26 the abnormal presence of virus or bacteria resulting in illness or disease
29 the inability to move part or all of the body; caused by illness, poisoning, or injury
32 nickname given to Mary Mallon, who was a carrier of Typhoid Fever
33 the contagious viral disease from which Old Yeller suffered; common in bats, coyotes, and skunks
36 a person who carries a disease that can be shared with their children genetically or by infecting others
37 microorganisms that cause disease

Medical Investigation 101 – Hill & Griffith

ACROSS

5 a parasitic disease transmitted by mosquitos; symptoms include recurring fever
6 an infectious and usually fatal disease characterized by fever and severe internal bleeding and spread by contact with infected body fluids; caused by a filovirus
9 a contagious bacterial disease that affects the lungs
11 having a fever
12 the acronym for human immunodefiency virus; there is currently no vaccine to prevent it
13 single-celled organisms that are neither bacteria or virus; an example is an Amoeba
16 a medicine used to stimulate anitbodies to provide immunity from a disease
18 a length equal to one-billionth of a meter
19 abnormal lateral curvature of the spine seen in female polio patients
20 virual disease killing more people in last 100 years that any other
23 a scientist who studies patterns of spreading of diseases
25 a medicine that inhibits the growth of bacteria
27 a disease that spreads throughout an entire country or around the world
28 developed a set of rules to prove specific germs caused specific diseases
30 a very thin layer of cells or material
31 the changing of genes from generation to generation for the purpose of adaptation
34 viral disease attacking the liver
35 organisms visible only under a microscope
38 tick-borne bacterial disease

Investigation 3.3A

Dr. _____

Rib Pain

P._____ Date_____

Vocabulary 1: Definitions

Directions: Use the text, a dictionary, or the internet to write a definition for each term.

1. fracture: _____
_____

2. appetite: _____
_____

3. depression: _____
_____

4. fibromyalgia: _____
_____

5. brachial plexus: _____
_____

6. stroke: _____
_____

7. multiple sclerosis: _____
_____

8. palpate: _____
_____

9. elicit: _____
_____

10. thorax: _____
_____

11. unilateral: _____
_____

12. bilateral: _____
_____

Investigation 3.3A Dr. _____

Rib Pain P._____ Date_____

Vocabulary 2: Matching

Directions: Match the definitions on the right to the terms on the left.

1. _____ fracture
2. _____ appetite
3. _____ depression
4. _____ fibromyalgia
5. _____ brachial plexus
6. _____ stroke
7. _____ multiple sclerosis
8. _____ palpate
9. _____ elicit
10. _____ thorax
11. _____ unilateral
12. _____ bilateral

a. a persistent feeling of sadness and lack of interest
b. to induce a reaction to a stimulus
c. a crack or break in a bone
d. the area of the body between the neck and abdomen
e. relating to or affecting both left and right sides
f. chronic musculoskeletal pain, fatigue, or tenderness on an area or areas
g. your desire and need for food
h. the network of nerves sending signals to and from your spine and shoulder, arm, and hand
i. to examine an area by touching
j. related to or affecting either right or left side, but not both sides
k. a progressive degenerative neurological disease causing numbness, speech impairment, fatigue, & loss of coordination
l. sudden death of brain cells due to arterial blockage or rupture

Investigation 3.3A

Rib Pain

Vocabulary 3: Sentences

Dr. _____

P._____ Date_____

Directions: Write a sentence using each term.

1. fracture: _____
   _____

2. appetite: _____
   _____

3. depression: _____
   _____

4. fibromyalgia: _____
   _____

5. brachial plexus: _____
   _____

6. stroke: _____
   _____

7. multiple sclerosis: _____
   _____

8. palpate: _____
   _____

9. elicit: _____
   _____

10. thorax: _____
    _____

11. unilateral: _____
    _____

12. bilateral: _____
    _____

Investigation 3.3A: Rib Area Pain   Dr. _____

Worksheet 3.3A1.4   P.____ Date:_____

Patient Workup

1. **Chief Complaint:** _____

2. **History of Chief Complaint:** (important points on present complaint)

    a. _____
    b. _____
    c. _____

3. **Review of Systems:** (list known past or present medical conditions)

    a. _____
    b. _____
    c. _____

4. **Examination:**

    Wt = ____ lbs.   Respirations: ____/min   Pulse: ____/min
    Blood Pressure: ____ / ____   Temperature = _____ ° F.

    Heart: _____

    Lungs: _____

    Chest exam:

    a. _____
    b. _____
    c. _____
    d. _____

    Why do you think the examination was limited to the chest area on this patient?

    _____
    _____

Investigation 3.3A: Rib Area Pain Dr. _____

Worksheet 3.3A1.4 - Patient Workup

Page 2

5. **Differential Diagnosis:**

Disorder	Acute/ Chronic	Pain ↑ moving/ breathing	Swollen lymph nodes	Head aches	rash	Uni or bi- lateral	Stiff joints	Numb ness	blisters	Dia- rhea
Muscle strain	A	X				U				
Rib Fracture	A	X				U		X		
Fibromyalgia	C	X		X		U/B	X			X
Food poisoning	A		X	X						X
Lung Cancer	C	X	X							
Brachial plexus injury	A	X				U		X		
Shingles	A/C		X		X	U			X	X
Stroke	A/C					U		X		
Multiple sclerosis	C	X				U/B				

6. **Medical Tests:** Which, if any, of the <u>following</u> tests would you have considered if Ed had returned to the office in two days with no change in his condition?

Summary of Available Tests to Consider and what information they can provide your medical investigation:

Which test(s) would be most appropriate at this time? (check any that apply)

_____ **X-rays** of the chest and ribs

_____ **MRI** of the chest and ribs

_____ **Rib Biopsy**

_____ **CBC** blood test

_____ **Ultrasound** of chest and ribs

_____ **Prescription** for pain medication

Investigation 3.3A: Rib Area Pain   Dr. _____

Worksheet 3.3A1.4 - Patient Workup   P.___ Date:_____

Page 3

7. **Treatment Options:**

Which treatment would be most appropriate while waiting for test results:

_____ **Emergency Surgery** to remove the painful rib.

_____ **Radiation therapy** to kill any cancer that may be starting to grow in the rib.

_____ **Prescription** for narcotic pain killer to allow patient to sleep for the next few nights until he returns for a progress check and more thorough examination.

_____ **Prescriptions for all antibiotics** that work on the four most common organisms causing infections.

_____ **No Treatment** until all tests come back with results on the cause of the pain.

8. **Test Results**

    What were the X-ray results received from the radiologist?
    _____
    _____

9. **Diagnosis: What is your Diagnosis?**
    _____

    What information led you to that diagnosis?
    _____
    _____
    _____
    _____
    _____
    _____

Investigation 3.3A: Rib Area Pain   Dr. _____

Worksheet 3.3A1.4 - Patient Workup

Page 4

10. Treatment Options:

Which treatment might you prescribe first? _____

Based on Ed's history and **symptoms** and your knowledge, is your step #1 treatment all that will be required?   Yes   No

Are there other treatment **modalities** that might be helpful in making your patient comfortable?   Yes   No

Select the treatment(s) below that would give your patient the best chance for relief in the **acute phase** of this disease

X if yes Blank if no	Treatment	purpose
	Acetaminophen	Pain management
	Oral antibiotics	Stop bacterial infection
	Oral Anti-viral meds	Stop viral infection
	Oral Corticosteroids	Stop inflammatory response in body
	Antibiotic cream	Stop skin infection in blisters
	Steroid cream	Stop inflammation of skin

Can shingles spread from one person to another? What about Shingles spreading Chicken Pox? If so, how? (You may have to read ahead in 3.3B to find the answers)

Method of spreading	yes	no
Through the air		
Blister to skin contact with another person who has had chicken pox		
Blister to skin contact with another person who has not had chicken pox		
Touching contaminated object		
Sharing a glass		
Contact with contaminated blood		
Contact with contaminated urine		
Cannot be spread to others		

Investigation 3.3A: Rib Area Pain   Dr. _____

Worksheet 3.3A2.5 - Reflections   P.___ Date:_____

Reflections:

What was your patient's chief complaint? _____

Would you consider Ed's complaint to be: (circle) Acute or Chronic

Why? _____

_____

_____

How would you classify Ed's condition (circle your answer)?

      Possible Emergency   or   Probably Non-Emergency

Which DDx possibilities did you **rule out** right away?

a. _____

b. _____

c. _____

Is Ed's condition an injury or illness? (Circle your answer)

If Ed's condition is an illness, is it **curable**? (circle answer)   Yes   No

Why or why not? _____

_____

_____

Was this injury or illness preventable? How or why not? _____

_____

_____

_____

Investigation 3.3A

Crossword 3.3A   **Rib Pain**

Dr._____

P.____ Date:_____

Directions: Use the highlighted terms in the chapter to solve the puzzle. Most clues come from the chapter text, some require outside investigation. Omit spaces or dashes between words.

Medical Investigation 101 - Hill & Griffith

ACROSS

1. a crack or break in a bone
3. a chronic disorder having symptoms of musculoskeletal pain, fatigue, and localized areas of tenderness
8. an autoimmune disease affecting the brain and spinal cord, causing impaired speech and muscle coordination
10. the part of the body located between the neck and the abdomen
11. temporary cessation of breathing, especially during sleep
13. occurs when blood flow to an area of the brain is disrupted by a clot or ruptured blood vessel
15. a group of symptoms that consistently occur together
18. feelings of severe despondency and dejection
20. a group of long, thin, curved bones that together make a boney cage that protects our vital organs
21. able to be felt on or within the body during an examinatiion
23. an instruction from a medical practitioner that authorizes a patient to receive a medicine or treatment
24. temporary unconsciousness caused by a blow to the head

DOWN

2. to cause an answer or response in reaction to an action or question
4. a feeling or worry or nervousness
5. a condition of inadequate hemoglobin in blood or deficiency of red blood cells causing fatigue and pallor
6. dysfunction of peripheral nerves causing numbness or weakness
7. the use of sound waves to examine the fetus during pregnancy
9. a network of nerves that control movement and sensation to the shoulder, arms, and hands
12. the desire to eat
14. to examine the body by touch
16. inability to produce enough insulin causing elevate blood sugar
17. an examination of tissue removed from a body to discover the presence or extent of a disease
19. skin eruption and acutely painful nerve inflammation caused by the chicken pox virus and occurring in older people who had chicken pox previously; preventable with a vaccine
22. accronym for computed tomography scan; uses x-rays to make detailed pictures of the inside of the body

Investigation 3.3B   Dr. _____

Shingles   P. _____ Date _____

Vocabulary 1: Definitions

Directions: Use the text, a dictionary, or the internet to write a definition for each term.

1. shingles: _____
   _____

2. chicken pox: _____
   _____

3. dormant: _____
   _____

4. blisters: _____
   _____

5. rash: _____
   _____

6. encephalitis: _____
   _____

7. vaccine: _____
   _____

8. neuralgia: _____
   _____

9. steroid: _____
   _____

10. transplant: _____
    _____

11. immune system: _____
    _____

12. preventable: _____
    _____

Investigation 3.3B

Shingles

Vocabulary 2: Matching

Directions: Match the definition on the right to the medical term on the left.

1. _____ shingles
2. _____ chicken pox
3. _____ dormant
4. _____ blisters
5. _____ rash
6. _____ encephalitis
7. _____ vaccine
8. _____ neuralgia
9. _____ steroid
10. _____ transplant
11. _____ immune system
12. _____ preventable

Dr. _____

P._____ Date_____

a. medicines used to reduce swelling and inflammation, such as cortisone

b. suspension or slowing of physical activities for a period of time

c. inflammation of the skin, often including redness and itching

d. an illness that can be prevented with a vaccine

e. childhood disease that can come back many years later as shingles

f. inflammation of the brain caused by infection or allergic reaction

g. small fluid-filled bubble on the skin caused by friction or burn

h. organs that can be replaced from a donor

i. preventable illness that can occur in those having had chicken pox

j. the system that protects the body from infection and disease

k. drugs that create immunity to specific bacteria or virus infections

l. intense pain along the course of a nerve

Investigation 3.3B　　　　　　　　　　　　　　　　　Dr. _____

Shingles　　　　　　　　　　　　　　　　　　　　　P._____ Date_____

Vocabulary 3: Sentences

Directions: Write a sentence using each medical term in the space provided.

1. shingles: _____
   _____

2. chicken pox: _____
   _____

3. dormant: _____
   _____

4. blisters: _____
   _____

5. rash: _____
   _____

6. encephalitis: _____
   _____

7. vaccine: _____
   _____

8. neuralgia: _____
   _____

9. steroid: _____
   _____

10. transplant: _____
    _____

11. immune system: _____
    _____

12. preventable: _____
    _____

Investigation 3.3B Dr. _____

Shingles Worksheet 3.3B.4 P.____Date:_____

Shingles

Directions: Answer the questions on your reading of Medical Investigation 3.3B.

1. Which virus causes chickenpox and shingles? _____

2. How can you protect yourself from contracting chickenpox?
   _____

3. How can your grandparents assure they do not contract Shingles?
   _____

4. What fraction of people over age 60 who had chicken pox earlier in life get Shingles?
   _____

5. How can the same virus that causes chickenpox in children and young adults cause shingles in grandparents? _____
   _____
   _____

6. Describe the order of steps of Shingles presentation in a patient who previously had chickenpox?
   _____
   _____
   _____

7. What are some of the rare complications that can occur in Shingles?
   _____
   _____

8. How old are most victims of Shingles?_____

9. What procedures can reduce the spread of the virus from Shingles blisters?
   _____
   _____

10. Which is more contagious, Shingles or Chickenpox? (circle your choice)

Investigation 3.3B Shingles

Crossword 3.3B.5: Shingles

Dr._____

P.____Date:_____

Directions: Use the highlighted terms in the chapter to solve the puzzle. Most clues come from the chapter text, but some require outside investigation. Omit spaces or dashes between words.

Medical Investigation 101 - Hill & Griffith

ACROSS

1. the ratio or fraction of chicken pox victims that develop Shingles years later
4. swellings filled with fluid on the surface of skin
6. lung inflammation caused by viral or bacterial infection
8. an injection of antibodies that can make you immune to a contagious disease
10. a potent anti-inflammatory medicine used to reduce pain and inflammation
14. the inability to see
15. intense pain along the course of a nerve
16. a change in skin color or texture, which may become bumpy, dry, blistered, painful or itchy

DOWN

2. surviving in an inactive state
3. the virus that causes Chicken Pox and Shingles
5. our lymphatic organs that help protect us from infdectiion; in some people weakness of this makes them more prone to sickness
7. able to catch a contagious disease
9. childhood contagious disease spread by varicella-zoster virus; can result in Shingles many years later
11. taking a healthy organ from one person and placing it surgically into another person
12. a viral illness in adults resulting from activation of a dormant varicella-zoster virus following a chicken pox infection
13. a preventive medicine containing antibodies to a specific contagious disease

Investigation 3.4A

Dr. _____

Sore Throat

P._____ Date_____

Vocabulary 1: Definitions

Directions: Use the text, a dictionary, or the internet to write a definition for each term.

1. erythema: _____
   _____

2. tympanic membrane: _____
   _____

3. tonsils: _____
   _____

4. purulent: _____
   _____

5. discharge: _____
   _____

6. abscess: _____
   _____

7. uvula: _____
   _____

8. lymph nodes: _____
   _____

9. reflexes: _____
   _____

10. pyrogen: _____
    _____

11. tonsillectomy: _____
    _____

12. pathogenic: _____
    _____

Investigation 3.4A   Dr. _____

Sore Throat   P._____ Date_____

Vocabulary 2: Matching

Directions: Match the definition on the right to the medical term on the left.

1. _____ erythema
2. _____ tympanic membrane
3. _____ tonsils
4. _____ purulent
5. _____ discharge
6. _____ abscess
7. _____ uvula
8. _____ lymph nodes
9. _____ reflexes
10. _____ pyrogen
11. _____ tonsillectomy
12. _____ pathogenic

a. fleshy structure that hangs downward in your throat; important functions in speech & swallowing
b. recommended surgical treatment for patients having several episodes of tonsillitis annually
c. redness of skin or tissue
d. the flow of fluid from an area of the body; example: a bloody nose
e. the cause of a fever; example: a bacteria
f. swollen area of tissue containing pus
g. movements made without conscious thought as reactions to stimuli.
h. lymphoid tissue on each side of the throat
i. capable of producing disease
j. consisting of or discharging pus
k. small gland-like masses that filter bacteria and foreign particles; swell when fighting infection
l. thin membrane that separates external and middle ear; vibrates to transmit sound waves

Investigation 3.4A

Sore Throat

Vocabulary 3: Sentences

Dr._____

P._____Date_____

Directions: Write a complete sentence using each term.

1. erythema: _____
_____

2. tympanic membrane: _____
_____

3. tonsils: _____
_____

4. purulent: _____
_____

5. discharge: _____
_____

6. abscess: _____
_____

7. uvula: _____
_____

8. lymph nodes: _____
_____

9. reflexes: _____
_____

10. pyrogen: _____
_____

11. tonsillectomy: _____
_____

12. pathogenic: _____
_____

Investigation 3.4A　　　　　　　　　　　　Dr._____

Workup Page 5　　　　　　　　　　　　　P.____Date:_____

Reflections

1. What was your patient's chief complaint? _____

2. Would you consider Ronald's complaint to be:

   　　　　　　(circle your answer)　　Acute　or　Chronic

3. Why? _____

4. How would you classify Ronald's condition (circle your answer)?

   　　　　　　Possible Emergency　or　Probably Non-Emergency

5. Which DDx possibilities did you **rule out** right away?

   a._____

   b._____

   c._____

   d._____

6. Was this an　injury　or　illness? (Circle your answer)

7. Was this injury or illness preventable? How or why not? _____
   _____
   _____
   _____
   _____
   _____
   _____

8. What is the normal range for red blood cells (rbc)? _____

9. What is the normal range for white blood cells (wbc)?_____

10. What test would you order to determine their RBC and WBC count?
    _____

Investigation 3.4A: Dr._____

11. Workup Page 6

12. What test is useful to determine which 'bug' is causing an infection?
_____

13. Why might you recommend a tonsillectomy for this patient? _____
_____

14. What was your Final Diagnosis?
_____

15. Why do you think Ronald developed a fever with his throat infection?
_____
_____
_____
_____

16. What is a "Pyrogen"? _____
_____

17. How does our body temperature influence the way pathogenic organism grow in our bodies?
_____
_____
_____
_____

Investigation 3.4A

Crossword 3.4A Sore Throat

Dr._____

P.____ Date:_____

Directions: Use the highlighted terms in the chapter to solve the puzzle. Most clues come from the chapter text, some require outside investigation. Omit spaces or dashes between words.

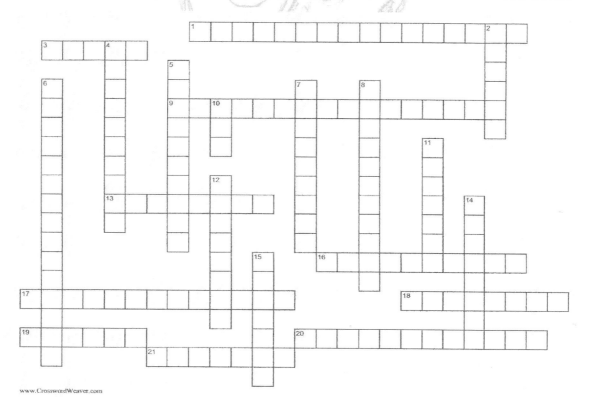

ACROSS

1. the treatment of disease, especially cancer, using X-rays and similar forms of radiation
3. fleshy structure that hangs from the roof of the mouth
9. thin tissue membrane separating middle ear and external ear; vibrates with sound, known as eardrum
13. reddening of tissue due to increase blood flow from irritation
16. use of high frequency sound waves to detect images withing the body
17. cells that contain hemoglobin and carry oxygen throughout the body
18. prevented or disqualified
19. the look when extra moisture forms on the eye and makes it look shiny
20. an instruction by a physician allowing a patient to have a treatment or medicine
21. the treatment of injury or illness by cutting open the body

DOWN

2. rythmical throbbing of arteries as blood travels through them
4. parts of the immune system that contain cells that trap cancer cells and bacteria
5. a medicine to stops the growth or kills bacteria
6. colorless cells in the body that help fight infection and disease
7. to flow out from an area of confinement
8. testing whether or not an antibiotic will stop or kill a bacteria causing an infection
10. abbreviation for magnetic resonance imaging; used to show layers of soft tissue structures within the body
11. two eval-shaped masses of tissue located on each side of the throat that trap germs and make antibodies to fight infection
12. reactions to stimuli that occur without conscience thought
14. consisting of, containing, or exuding pus
15. growing bacteria in an artificial environment

105

Investigation 3.4B

Dr. _____

Role of Blood

P.____ Date_____

Vocabulary 1: Definitions

Directions: Use the text, a dictionary, or the internet to write a definition for each term.

1. blood: _____
_____

2. plasma: _____
_____

3. white blood cells: _____
_____

4. platelets: _____
_____

5. red blood cells: _____
_____

6. centrifuge: _____
_____

7. suspend: _____
_____

8. transfusion: _____
_____

9. hemophilia: _____
_____

10. allergen: _____
_____

11. hemoglobin: _____
_____

12. Sickle Cell Anemia: _____
_____

Investigation 3.4B

Role of Blood

Vocabulary 2: Matching

Dr._____

P.____Date_____

Directions: Match each definition at the right to the medical term on the left.

1. _____ blood
2. _____ plasma
3. _____ white blood cells
4. _____ platelets
5. _____ red blood cells
6. _____ centrifuge
7. _____ suspend
8. _____ transfusion
9. _____ hemophilia
10. _____ allergen
11. _____ hemoglobin
12. _____ Sickle Cell Anemia

a. lymphocytes, monocytes, basophils, neutrophils, and eosinophils
b. hemoglobin-containing cells that carry oxygen and carbon dioxide
c. substance causing allergic reaction
d. severe hereditary anemia where red blood cells are crescent shaped
e. the liquid component of blood
f. the component of blood responsible for carrying oxygen
g. transfer of blood or its components from one person to another
h. the liquid that flows in arteries and veins, carrying oxygen and carbon dioxide
i. a machine applying centrifugal force to separate fluids of different densities or solids from liquids
j. the component of blood that assists in clotting of blood
k. hereditary disorder where ability of blood to clot is severely reduced
l. all blood components spread evenly throughout the blood sample

Investigation 3.4B

Role of Blood

Vocabulary 3: Sentences

Dr. _____

P. ____ Date _____

Directions: Use the text, a dictionary, or the internet to write a definition for each term.

1. blood: _____
   _____

2. plasma: _____
   _____

3. white blood cells: _____
   _____

4. platelets: _____
   _____

5. red blood cells: _____
   _____

6. centrifuge: _____
   _____

7. suspend: _____
   _____

8. transfusion: _____
   _____

9. hemophilia: _____
   _____

10. allergen: _____
    _____

11. hemoglobin: _____
    _____

12. Sickle Cell Anemia: _____
    _____

Investigation 3.4B1 Dr._____

Blood Worksheet, page 1 P: ___Date:_____

Directions: Use the information you learned about blood to answer the following questions.

1. What are the three major components of blood?

    a. _____

    b. _____

    c. _____

2. What do we call the process by which we stop bleeding when we get a cut?

    _____

3. Which component of blood contains clotting factors?

    _____

4. What is the name of the disease where clotting factors are absent?

    _____

5. What is the liquid part of blood called?

    _____

6. List the five types of white blood cells.

    a. _____

    b. _____

    c. _____

    d. _____

    e. _____

7. Why is it important that we have white blood cells?

    _____

    _____

Investigation 3.4B1 Dr._____
Blood Worksheet, page 2

Which white blood cells signal the other cells to attack?

_____

8. Which white blood cells are immediately dispatched to fight infection; they are the largest of the white blood cells?

_____

9. Which white blood cells prevent blood clots from forming too quickly?

_____

10. Which white blood cells provide our main source of 'immunity'?

_____

11. Which white blood cells promote blood flow to the injured area of your body?

_____

12. Which component of blood does NOT need to be tested for blood type before transfusing into a patient?

_____

13. What is the other name for red blood cells?

_____

14. What component of the red blood cell carries oxygen and carbon dioxide?

_____

Investigation 3.4B1 – Reflections

Blood Worksheet, page 3

Dr._____

P.____ Date:_____

15. Where do red blood cells exchange oxygen for carbon dioxide?

    _____

16. About what percent of your blood is made up of platelets and white blood cells?

    _____%

17. In which genetic disease are the red blood cells misshaped such that it is difficult for them to carry oxygen?

    _____

18. Write a paragraph about Sickle Cell Anemia. Research information on the internet and provide evidence from your resources to back up your statements.

    _____
    _____
    _____
    _____
    _____
    _____
    _____
    _____
    _____
    _____
    _____
    _____

Investigation 3.4B1 – Reflections
Blood Worksheet, **page 4**

Dr._____

Art Project: 1. Draw a picture that demonstrates all of the components of blood. 2. Then, draws two red blood cells side by side. The first should be a normal red blood cell and the second a sickled red blood cell. Label every cell in each drawing.

Draw and label all of the components of blood in the box below:

Draw normal red blood cells on the left and sickled red blood cells on the right:

Investigation 3.4B　　　　　　　　　　　　　　Dr._____

Crossword 3.4B　　　　**Role of Blood**　　P._____Date:_____

Directions: Use the highlighted terms in the chapter to solve the puzzle. Most clues come from the chapter text, but some require outside investigation. Omit spaces or dashes between words.

Medical Investigation 101 – Hill & Griffith

ACROSS

1. when blood cell components float around in plasma without dropping to the bottom
2. red blood cells that have been collected, separated, and stored in bags for transfusion to patients in need
4. the most abundant white blood cells that represent your body's first line of defense
6. also called erythrocytes; a solid component of blood that carries oxygen and carbon dioxide to and from tissues
8. WBCs that prevent blood from clotting too quickly and stimulate blood flow to injured area
10. our main immunity cells; provide sustained attacks on pathogens and allergens
13. the breathe out
17. the component of blood that controls the clotting process
21. the ability of blood to stop bleeding
22. large molecules that are essential in hair, muscles, and other body tissues
24. specific part of red blood cell that binds oxygen to carry to tissues
26. to roughly calculate or judge something's value
27. the person who provides the blood cmponent to be given to another person
28. there are thirteen of these that work to stop bleeding

DOWN

1. abnormal blood condition where red blood cells are misshaped in the form of a sickle
3. the smallest blood vessels; where oxygen and carbon dioxide exchange occurs in tissues
5. moving blood components from one person to another
7. known as leucocytes, they represent our body's major defense against infection
9. chemicals or poisons that are harmful to your body
11. measuring the similarities or differences between two things
12. waste product gas carried back to lungs to be exhaled
14. a spinning machine used to separate fluids of different densities
15. a hereditary condition where there is reduced ability to clot blood, causing severe bleeding even with minor cuts
16. the WBC's that signal other white blood cells to attack infections or allergens
18. substances that cause allergic reactions
19. the largest white blood cells, immediately attack pathogens
20. carried by red blood cells; produces energy in our tissues
23. the almost colorless part of blood in which red and white blood cells are suspended
25. fluid that circulates through arteries and veins, carrying oxygen and carbon dioxide to and from body tissues

Investigation 3.5A

Dr. _____

Emergencies

P. _____ Date _____

Vocabulary 1: Definitions

Directions: Use the text, a dictionary, or the internet to write a definition for each term.

1. emergency: _____
   _____

2. basic life support: _____
   _____

3. Red Cross: _____
   _____

4. CAB: _____
   _____

5. lactic acid: _____
   _____

6. Blood Bank: _____
   _____

7. Scoop and Run: _____
   _____

8. heart attack: _____
   _____

9. respiration: _____
   _____

10. choking: _____
    _____

11. trachea: _____
    _____

12. Heimlich Maneuver: _____
    _____

Investigation 3.5A

Emergencies

Vocabulary 2: Matching

Dr. _____

P. _____ Date _____

Directions: Match the explanation at the right to the medical term on the left.

1. _____ emergency
2. _____ basic life support
3. _____ Red Cross
4. _____ CAB
5. _____ lactic acid
6. _____ blood bank
7. _____ scoop and run
8. _____ heart attack
9. _____ respiration
10. _____ choking
11. _____ trachea
12. _____ Heimlich Maneuver

a. the concept of getting the injured to the hospital as quickly as possible without treating in the field
b. sudden damage to the heart muscle, usually caused by blockage of an artery within the heart
c. any condition requiring immediate treatment to prevent death or permanent disability
d. procedure for dislodging an object from a person's windpipe
e. a place where blood is stored until needed for transfusion
f. non-invasive emergency procedures to assist immediate survival of a patient
g. organization having mission to care for sick and wounded, and relieve suffering
h. forms in muscle tissue during strenuous activity
i. difficulty breathing due to airway blockage
j. order of emergency life support: chest compression, airway, breathing
k. breathing in oxygen and exhaling carbon dioxide
l. the windpipe that carries oxygen to the lungs

Investigation 3.5A

Emergencies

Vocabulary 3: Sentences

Dr. _____

P._____ Date _____

Directions: Use each term in a sentence.

1. emergency: _____
   _____

2. basic life support: _____
   _____

3. Red Cross: _____
   _____

4. CAB: _____
   _____

5. lactic acid: _____
   _____

6. Blood Bank: _____
   _____

7. Scoop and Run: _____
   _____

8. heart attack: _____
   _____

9. respiration: _____
   _____

10. choking: _____
    _____

11. trachea: _____
    _____

12. Heimlich Maneuver: _____
    _____

Investigation 3.5A Dr. _____

Emergencies P:___ Date:_____

Emergencies Worksheet

1. What course can you and a friend or family member take to learn basic skills that could save a life in an emergency?
   _____

2. Name two organizations who sponsor Basic Life Support training that you can contact to schedule a class?

   a. _____
   b. _____

3. What is the first thing you should do when coming upon an obvious medical emergency?
   _____

4. What do the letters CAB stand for in the order of basic life support?

   a. _____
   b. _____
   c. _____

5. When your body produces energy while you are unable to breath, what toxic chemical accumulates in your blood?
   _____

6. If you come upon a non-responsive person lying on the ground and you cannot detect a pulse, what is the first thing you should do after calling 911?
   _____

7. Should you come upon a person who is bleeding profusely, what can you do to help keep them from bleeding to death?
   _____

Worksheet 3.5A: Emergencies	Dr._____
Page 2

8. Basic Life Support classes teach you how to respond when you come upon someone suffering from what possible scenarios:

   a. _____
   b. _____
   c. _____
   d. _____
   e. _____

9. If you are visiting your grandmother and she suffers a sudden loss of her vision, speech, or sudden muscle weakness, what should you do?

   _____

10. In the above situation, what might be happening to your grandmother?

    _____

11. What is the "time window" to get a stroke victim to a hospital to give the best chance of survival with the least long-term disability?

    _____

12. When someone is brought to the emergency room with severe bleeding, what is the emergency doctor likely to order?

    _____

13. Where does the emergency room get blood for transfusions?

    _____

Worksheet 3.5A: Emergencies   Dr._____

Page 3   P:___ Date:_____

14. When someone at the dinner table suddenly cannot talk and grabs their throat, what is probably happening?
    _____

15. What is the medical term for "wind pipe"?
    _____

16. What is the name of the technique used to expel food lodged in the wind pipe by squeezing the victim's abdomen?
    _____

17. Why do choking victims never yell for help?
    _____

18. Why is the term "Heart Attack" an inadequate explanation of a heart problem?
    _____
    _____

19. What is a 'Myocardial Infarction"?
    _____

20. Which sensors located in the heart recognize an inadequate oxygen supply and cause a reduction in blood flow to non-vital organs?
    _____

Worksheet 3.5A: Emergencies   Dr._____

Page 4

21. What is ventricular fibrillation?
_____
_____

22. What can be done to help a person suffering ventricular fibrillation?
_____

23. How would you know how to use a defibrillator you find and need to use at school if no adult is around?
_____
_____

24. If someone in your home experiences sudden chest pain spreading into their left arm or their jaw, what should you do?
_____
Why?_____

25. Do you need to be 21 years old to become certified in Basic Life Support?

    NO   YES   (circle your choice)

26. How is myocardial infarction different from ventricular fibrillation? (2 ways)
    a. _____
    b. _____

Investigation 3.5A

Crossword — Emergencies

Dr._____
P.____ Date:_____

Directions: Use the highlighted terms in the chapter to solve the puzzle. Most clues come from the chapter text, some require outside investigation. Omit spaces or dashes between words.

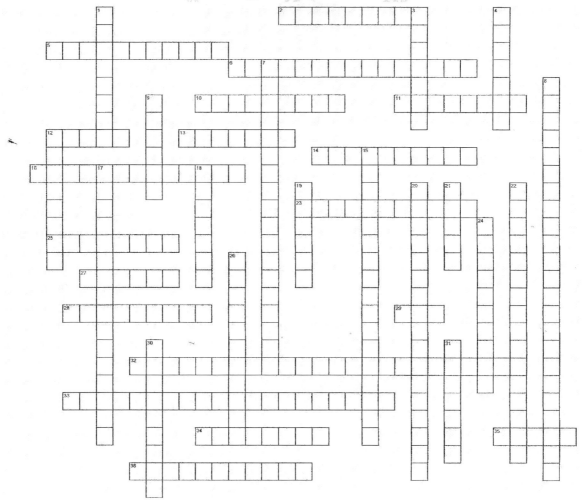

Medical Investigation 101 - Hill & Griffith

ACROSS

- 2 how we move air into our lungs
- 5 sudden chest pain or sudden loss of a pulse
- 6 no effective respiration or chest movement
- 10 the place where blood for transfusions is stored until it is needed
- 11 what follows when an artery or vein is cut or ruptures
- 12 the rate of our heart beat
- 13 made weaker or reduced in concentration
- 14 audible instructions in the operation of a defibrillator such that anyone can correctly shock a victim back to life
- 16 a device that can restore a regular heart beat in patients with ventricular fibrillation
- 23 what we give patients who have lost enough blood that their blood pressure is too low
- 25 organization having emergency skills certification
- 27 what needs to be open in order to get air into the lungs
- 28 things that reverse or minimize the effects of a stroke
- 29 acronym for order of priorities in administering emergency skills: circulation, airway, breathing
- 32 the organization that found children 9 years old can adminster life-saving skills
- 33 when heart muscle cells die from blockage of an oxygen-carrying artery
- 34 not critical to life itself
- 35 shorter version of the paramedic
- 36 the name given to the process of getting the patient to the hospital as soon as possible without treating them at the scene of the emergency

DOWN

- 1 who can stop the bleeding once the patient has been moved to the hospital?
- 3 what you should do before starting to act in an emergency
- 4 something blocking the air passage to the lungs; can occur when we don't chew our food adequately or take enormous bites
- 7 when a patient imply falls down with no pulse
- 8 the class of heart attack where the heart beats out of normal rhythm and no longer pumps blood effectively
- 9 the process of breathing out; choking victims cannot do this
- 12 what you should apply to a bleeding blood vessel
- 15 the first step in administering emergency basic life support; do not stop until help arrives
- 17 we should all earn this certification; it could enable us to save someone's life
- 18 structure directing air from mouth towards lungs
- 19 sudden weakness or impaired speech
- 20 nerve endings in the heart that sense a lack of oxygen
- 21 poisonous or harmful
- 22 the procedure that is effective in helping choking victims
- 24 produced during our body's alternative method of releasing energy; toxic to cells if it builds up
- 26 the way we move oxygen throughout our bodies
- 30 a serious, unexpected situation requiring immediate action
- 31 what you should do on your telephone before aministering your emergency skills

Investigation 3.5B

Dr. _____

Chest Pain

P. _____ Date _____

Vocabulary 1: Definitions

Directions: Use the text, a dictionary, or the internet to write a definition for each term.

1. myocardial infarction: _____
   _____

2. angina: _____
   _____

3. aortic dissection: _____
   _____

4. pericarditis: _____
   _____

5. radiates: _____
   _____

6. costochondritis: _____
   _____

7. cartilage: _____
   _____

8. pleurisy: _____
   _____

9. inspiration: _____
   _____

10. collapsed lung: _____
    _____

11. panic attack: _____
    _____

12. shingles: _____
    _____

Investigation 3.5B

Chest Pain

Vocabulary 2: Matching

Dr. _____

P._____Date_____

Directions: Match the definitions on the right to the medical terms on the left.

1. _____ myocardial infarction
2. _____ angina
3. _____ aortic dissection
4. _____ pericarditis
5. _____ radiates
6. _____ costochondritis
7. _____ cartilage
8. _____ pleurisy
9. _____ inspiration
10. _____ collapsed lung
11. _____ panic attack
12. _____ shingles

a. sudden feeling of disabling anxiety
b. tearing of the inner layer of aorta
c. breathing in air
d. pain that spreads away from the starting point
e. strong, bendable tissue found in your nose and external ears, also lines joints
f. acute chest pain caused by inadequate heart blood supply
g. inflammation of the cartilage connecting the ribs to the sternum
h. death of heart muscle tissue occurring in a heart attack
i. buildup of air between lung and chest wall causing progressive breathing difficulty
j. inflammation of the outer covering of the lungs
k. painful condition stimulated by re-activation of chicken pox virus years later
l. inflammation of the outer covering of the heart

Investigation 3.5B

Chest Pain

Vocabulary 3: Sentences

Dr. _____

P. _____ Date _____

Directions: Write a sentence using each term.

1. myocardial infarction: _____
   _____

2. angina: _____
   _____

3. aortic dissection: _____
   _____

4. pericarditis: _____
   _____

5. radiates: _____
   _____

6. costochondritis: _____
   _____

7. cartilage: _____
   _____

8. pleurisy: _____
   _____

9. inspiration (medical use): _____
   _____

10. collapsed lung: _____
    _____

11. panic attack: _____
    _____

12. shingles (not on a roof): _____
    _____

Investigation 3.5B   Dr. _____

Chest Pain Worksheet   P: ___ Date: _____

Chest Pain Worksheet

1. **True or False**: In well over half of all emergency room visits for chest pain the final diagnosis is "myocardial infarction".

2. Name five major categories of chest pain:
   a. _____
   b. _____
   c. _____
   d. _____
   e. _____

3. Name four causes of cardiac chest pain:
   a. _____
   b. _____
   c. _____
   d. _____

4. What is a myocardial infarction?
   _____
   _____

5. What is Angina?
   _____
   _____

6. What causes patients to feel Angina?
   _____

Worksheet 3.5B: Chest Pain   Dr._____

Page 2

7. What is Aortic Dissection?
_____
_____

8. What is the pericardium?
_____

9. What is pericarditis?
_____

10. Why is pericarditis a dangerous condition?
_____
_____

11. What does the esophagus connect?
_____

12. What causes heartburn?
_____
_____
_____

13. Why do disorders of the gall bladder and pancreas cause chest pain?
_____
_____
_____

Worksheet 3.5B: Chest Pain   Dr._____

Page 3   P:___ Date:_____

14. Costochondritis represents injury to what body structure(s)?
    _____

15. Besides your heart, which other major organ is located in the chest?
    _____

16. What is a pulmonary embolism?
    _____
    _____

17. What complication can occur in the presence of pulmonary hypertension?
    _____

18. During which part of the respiratory cycle does the patient have pain in Pleurisy?
    _____

19. Name two non-specific origins of chest pain:
    a. _____
    b. _____

20. What technique does an emergency room doctor use to make the diagnosis for a patient with chest pain?
    _____
    _____

Investigation 3.5B: Chest Pain

Dr._____

Page 4

P.____ Date_____

21. Write a paragraph about someone in your family who experienced chest pain or visited the emergency room for another reason. Write your impressions of their experience.

Investigation 3.5B

Crossword 3.5B — **Chest Pain**

Dr._____

P.____Date:_____

Directions: Use the highlighted terms in the chapter to solve the puzzle. Most clues come from the chapter text, some require outside investigation. Omit spaces or dashes between words.

Medical Investigation 101 - Hill & Griffith

ACROSS

1 fibrous tissue that cushions bones at joints; its degradation causes osteoarthritis
3 occurs when a bood clot becomes trapped in a lung artery
7 when stress causes a person to feel chest pain, rapid heart beat, or difficulty breathing
9 referring to the heart
11 the protective sac or covering of the heart
13 the condition where the protective membrane surrounding the heart becomes infected or inflamed
14 when air leaks out of a lung and into the space between the lung and ribs
15 the flat bone located in the center of your chest; forms the front of the rib cage
17 small sac-shaped organ that stores bile after its secretion by the liver
18 chest pain stimulated by ischemic receptors
19 a rupture of the aorta
20 a condition where the outer covering of the lungs becomes inflamed; can make breathing in painful
21 caused by varicella-zoster virus in patients having had chicken pox years ago
22 condition where the pressure in the arteries leading to the lungs is above normal; can lead to fluid accumulation in the lungs

DOWN

2 the the long, thin, curved bones that together make a cage that protects the vital organs
4 means death of heart muscle; results from blockage of arteries within the heart that supply oxygen to the heart
5 fibrous tissue that contracts to produce movement of stability of body parts
6 pain that spreads away from its point of origin
8 the act of breathing in air
10 inflammation of the cartilage joining to the sternum
12 a large gland located behind the stomach; secretes digestive enzymes such as glucagon and insulin
16 occurs when acid backwashes from thestomach and irritates the inside of the esophagus

Investigation 3.6A

Dr. _____

Chronic Disease

P._____ Date_____

Vocabulary 1: Definitions

Directions: Use the text, a dictionary, or the internet to write a definition for each term.

1. obesity: _____
   _____

2. carbohydrates: _____
   _____

3. protein: _____
   _____

4. fat: _____
   _____

5. type II diabetes: _____
   _____

6. consultation: _____
   _____

7. percussion (as used in a medical examination): _____
   _____

8. bowel sounds: _____
   _____

9. distention: _____
   _____

10. hemoglobin A1C: _____
    _____

11. type 1 diabetes: _____
    _____

12. genetic abnormality: _____
    _____

Investigation 3.6A

Chronic Disease

Vocabulary 2: Matching

Dr. _____

P._____Date_____

Directions: Match the definitions on the right to the terms on the left.

1. _____ obesity
2. _____ carbohydrates
3. _____ protein
4. _____ fat
5. _____ type II diabetes
6. _____ consultation
7. _____ percussion
8. _____ bowel sounds
9. _____ distention
10. _____ hemoglobin A1C
11. _____ type 1 diabetes
12. _____ genetic abnormality

a. essential long chains of amino acids; examples include hair and finger/toenails
b. enlarged or swollen from too much internal pressure
c. chronic condition where pancreas produces little or no insulin
d. adipose tissue; typically stored beneath skin or around organs
e. severely overweight; a huge problem associated with over-eating
f. examination technique using tapping to determine size, texture, and shape of organs
g. test that determines average blood sugar concentrations over 2 to 3 months
h. congenital problem caused by abnormality within the genes
i. food group that includes sugars and starches; includes potatoes, pasta, bread, candy
j. normal grumbling sounds from the abdomen caused by peristalsis
k. an examination performed at the request of another physician
l. chronic condition where insulin is made, but not utilized efficiently

Investigation 3.6A　　　　　　　　　　　　　　　　　　Dr. _____

Chronic Disease　　　　　　　　　　　　　　　　　　　P._____Date_____

Vocabulary 3: Sentences

Directions: Write a sentence using each word.

1. obesity: _____
   _____

2. carbohydrates: _____
   _____

3. protein: _____
   _____

4. fat: _____
   _____

5. type II diabetes: _____
   _____

6. consultation: _____
   _____

7. percussion: _____
   _____

8. bowel sounds: _____
   _____

9. distention: _____
   _____

10. hemoglobin A1C: _____
    _____

11. type 1 diabetes: _____
    _____

12. genetic abnormality: _____
    _____

Investigation 3.6A Dr. _____

Worksheet 3.6A P.____Date:_____

Title: Diabetes Workup

Directions: Use the information from your reading to complete your diabetes workup on this patient.

Patient Name: _____ Age: _____ Gender: M F

Vital Signs: **Ht**: _____in **Wt**: _____lbs **BP**: _____ mmHg **Pulse**: ____ b/m Temp: _____ F

CC: Referred for diabetic control in preparation for left knee replacement surgery

HxCC: (List important information from patient in history of chief complaint)

 1. _____
 2. _____
 3. _____

ROS: (List all positive findings from Review of Records)- list additional positives on back)

 1. _____
 2. _____

Positive Examination Findings:

 1. _____
 2. _____
 3. _____
 4. _____

DDX:

 1. _____
 2. _____
 3. _____

Worksheet 3.6A – Workup   Dr._____

Page 2

Place an 'X' on the line next to any test you would consider at this time to help your investigation of this patient's medical problem. Write <u>NA</u> for any test listed that is probably not appropriate to your evaluation of this condition:

    _____   X-rays of abdomen including pancreas and liver

    _____   Complete Blood Count (CBC)

    _____   MRI of the pancreas and liver

    _____   Ultrasound of Pancreas and Liver

    _____   Repeat A1C blood test

Lab Test Results:

The following chart represents the key to reading Hemoglobin A1C test results:

Diabetes Diagnosis	Hemoglobin A1C level in blood
Normal (non-diabetic)	Less than (<) 5.7%
Pre-diabetic	Between 5.7% and 6.4%
Diabetes	6.5% or greater
Gilbert's 2nd A1C results	****7.7%****

A1C Lab Test Difference: What are some possible explanations as to the difference between the A1C test ordered by Dr. Drazer and the second test ordered by you?

1. _____

2. _____

3. _____

Diagnosis. (Hint: Find them on the DDX list)

1. _____

2. _____

Treatment Recommendations: What is the order of progressive treatment for Type II Diabetes?

1. _____

2. _____

3. _____

Worksheet 3.6A – Workup   Dr._____

Page 3   P.___ Date:_____

Check the appropriate box to indicate how <u>this medical condition</u> spreads from one person to another (more than one method of spreading may exist):

Method of spreading	yes	no
Through the air		
Skin to skin contact with another person		
Touching contaminated object		
Genetic sharing within families		
Contact with contaminated blood		
Drinking contaminated water		
Contact with contaminated urine		
Cannot be spread to friends		

Interview someone you know who has diabetes. Are they related to you? From your observations do they look any different from others you know who are not diabetic? What type of diabetes do they have and what is their treatment regimen? How has having diabetes changed their life? What do they do to keep their diabetes under control? (Continue on back of page if needed)

_____
_____
_____
_____
_____
_____
_____
_____
_____
_____
_____
_____

Worksheet 3.6A – Workup   Dr._____

Page 4

Reflections:

1. What was your patient's (Gilbert) chief complaint?
   _____
   _____

2. Would you consider Gilbert's complaint to be: (circle) **Acute or Chronic**
   Why? _____

3. How would you classify Gilbert's condition (circle your answer)?

   Possible Emergency   or   Probably Non-Emergency

4. Was this an **injury or illness**? (Circle your answer)

5. Was this injury or illness preventable? How or why not?
   _____
   _____
   _____
   _____
   _____

6. What is considered the normal range for an A1C blood test? _____

7. List some of the symptoms Gilbert exhibited before he was diagnosed as having diabetes.

   a. _____
   b. _____
   c. _____
   d. _____

8. What test would you order to determine if your patient is normal, pre-diabetic, or diabetic? _____

Worksheet 3.6A – Workup   Dr._____

Page 5   P.___Date:_____

9. What is happening within the body in Type I Diabetes?

   _____

   _____

10. What is happening within the body in Type II Diabetes?

    _____

    _____

11. How many types of Diabetes have been identified to date?

    _____

12. Do you think Gilbert's weight of 270 pounds before he developed Type II Diabetes could have been a factor in his current left knee condition? How?

    _____

    _____

    _____

    _____

13. Which of the following are questions that should have been asked of Gilbert during his first visit back to your office following his referral from Dr. Drazer? (put an 'X' beside each appropriate question)

    a. _____ Have you had your knee implant surgery yet?

    b. _____ Have you changed your diet recently?

    c. _____ Is your knee feeling better with the medicine I gave you?

    d. _____ Have you been taking your diabetic medicine regularly and in the correct dose?

    e. _____ Have you checked your blood pressure at home recently?

    f. _____ Have you noticed a lump on your pancreas recently?

Worksheet 3.6A – Workup Dr._____

Page 6

14. Write about the known effects of diabetes on the human body. Use your current knowledge and the internet to research the topic.

_____
_____
_____
_____
_____
_____
_____
_____
_____
_____
_____
_____
_____
_____
_____
_____
_____
_____
_____
_____

Investigation 3.6B

Dr. _____

Diabetes

P. _____ Date _____

Vocabulary 1: Definitions

Directions: Use the text, a dictionary, or the internet to write a definition for each term.

1. diabetes: _____
   _____

2. culture (as used medically): _____
   _____

3. preventable: _____
   _____

4. complications: _____
   _____

5. neuropathy: _____
   _____

6. retinopathy: _____
   _____

7. gangrene: _____
   _____

8. hemorrhage: _____
   _____

9. ophthalmoscope: _____
   _____

10. Islets of Langerhans: _____
    _____

11. alpha cells: _____
    _____

12. beta cells: _____
    _____

Investigation 3.6B

Diabetes

Vocabulary 2: Matching

Dr. _____

P_____ Date_____

Directions: Match the definitions on the right to the medical terms on the left.

1. _____ diabetes
2. _____ culture
3. _____ preventable
4. _____ complications
5. _____ neuropathy
6. _____ retinopathy
7. _____ gangrene
8. _____ hemorrhage
9. _____ ophthalmoscope
10. _____ Islets of Langerhans
11. _____ alpha cells
12. _____ beta cells

a. instrument for examining the interior of the eye, especially the retina
b. side effects or undesirable outcomes of treatment or recovery from an injury or illness
c. pancreatic cells that produce glucagon
d. chronic disease where pancreas produces too little insulin or insulin not effectively utilized
e. death of tissue from lack of blood supply
f. an unnecessary illness or injury
g. the type of pancreatic cells that produce insulin
h. injury or disease of retina resulting in loss of or diminished vision
i. the area of the pancreas where insulin is produced
j. growing bacteria to determine its identity and which antibiotic will be effective
k. diminished sensitivity of peripheral nerves caused by injury or disease
l. heavy discharge of blood from an artery or vein

Investigation 3.6B Dr. _____

Diabetes P_____ Date_____

Vocabulary 3: Sentences

Directions: Write a complete sentence using each word.

1. diabetes: _____
   _____

2. culture: _____
   _____

3. preventable: _____
   _____

4. complications: _____
   _____

5. neuropathy: _____
   _____

6. retinopathy: _____
   _____

7. gangrene: _____
   _____

8. hemorrhage: _____
   _____

9. ophthalmoscope: _____
   _____

10. Islets of Langerhans: _____
    _____

11. alpha cells: _____
    _____

12. beta cells: _____
    _____

Investigation 3.6B   Dr._____

Worksheet 1: Diabetes   P. ___ Date:_____

Diabetes

1. What is diabetes?
   _____
   _____

2. What percent of the American population suffers from diabetes?
   _____

3. Does one's culture have the potential to affect their risk of developing type 2 diabetes? (Circle your answer)   YES   NO   In what ways? (describe below)
   _____
   _____

4. Is the occurrence of Diabetes in the United States increasing or decreasing?
   _____

5. What other disturbing health occurrence that affects the rates of diabetes has an upward trend in the United States?
   _____

6. Is type 1 diabetes preventable?   Yes   No

7. Is type 2 diabetes preventable?   Yes   No

8. What is the number one factor in the upward trend of diabetes? _____

9. What are the two most important factors in the upward trend in obesity?
   a. _____
   b. _____

10. List <u>five</u> things a patient can do to reduce their risk of diabetes.
    a. _____
    b. _____
    c. _____
    d. _____
    e. _____

Investigation 3.6B: Diabetes Dr. _____

Worksheet 1, Page 2

11. What is the number one influence on a person's diet? _____

12. Describe how physicians are also teachers. _____
_____
_____

13. Name seven or more complications that attack your diabetic patient's health.

    1. _____
    2. _____
    3. _____
    4. _____
    5. _____
    6. _____
    7. _____
    8. _____
    9. _____

14. Which two hormones produced in the pancreas regulate your body's blood sugar levels?
_____ _____

15. What is the basic function of insulin? _____
_____

16. What is the basic function of glucagon? _____
_____

17. In which pancreatic cells are insulin and glucagon produced? _____
_____

18. Where within the abdominal cavity is the pancreas located?
_____

19. What medical instrument is useful to evaluate the condition of your diabetic patient's retina?
_____

Investigation 3.6B: Diabetes　　　　　　　　　　　　Dr._____

Worksheet 3.6B2: Diabetes　　　**Vocabulary Match**　　　P.____ Date:_____

Directions: Place the letter of the definition in the space provided on the left of the medical term.

1. _____ Diabetes
2. _____ Ethnicity
3. _____ Preventable
4. _____ Dietary practices
5. _____ Complications
6. _____ Preventive measures
7. _____ Educator
8. _____ Glucose
9. _____ Capillary
10. _____ Neuropathy
11. _____ Retinopathy
12. _____ Gangrene
13. _____ Retina
14. _____ Hemorrhages
15. _____ Regulate
16. _____ Islets of Langerhans
17. _____ Insulin
18. _____ glucagon

a. Problems that arise during an illness or from the treatment that add to your patient's suffering.
b. Hormone produced in pancreas that indirectly raises blood sugar
c. Structure of the eye where the image seen is focused
d. Things you and your patients can do to prevent illness
e. Your family heritage, based on your ancestors
f. Black tissue that is dead from infection or lack of blood supply
g. The things you choose to eat
h. When blood leaks out of capillaries and other blood vessels
i. The cells in the pancreas where insulin is produced
j. A disease where the body does not maintain a proper balance of blood glucose
k. The ability to control, such as maintaining the appropriate blood glucose range
l. The medical name for sugar when it is in the blood
m. The hormone produced in the pancreas responsible for lowering blood sugar
n. When the sensory or motor nerves have diminished function
o. Things you can stop before they happen
p. When the capillaries in the back of the eye leak blood onto the retina
q. You, as a doctor, are also a teacher or _____
r. Very small blood vessels where oxygen and nutrients enter cells

Investigation 3.6B - Diabetes Dr._____

Worksheet 3.6B3: Diabetic Complications P.____Date:_____

Directions: Write the name of each <u>diabetic complication</u> in the space provided next to its number from the diagram.

1. _____
2. _____
3. _____
4. _____
5. _____
6. _____
7. _____
8. _____
9. _____
10. _____

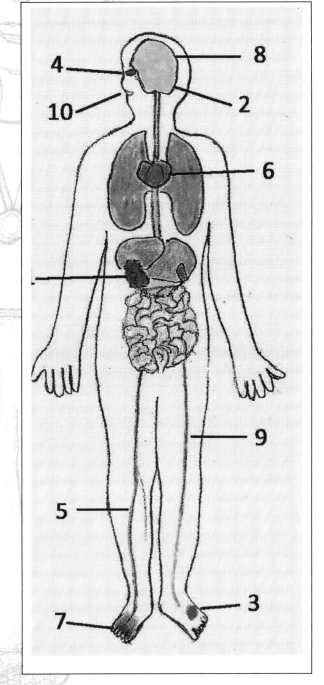

145

Investigation 3.6B - Diabetes Dr._____

Worksheet 3.6B4: Abdominal Organs P.____Date:_____

Directions: Write the name of each abdominal organ in the space provided next to its number from the diagram.

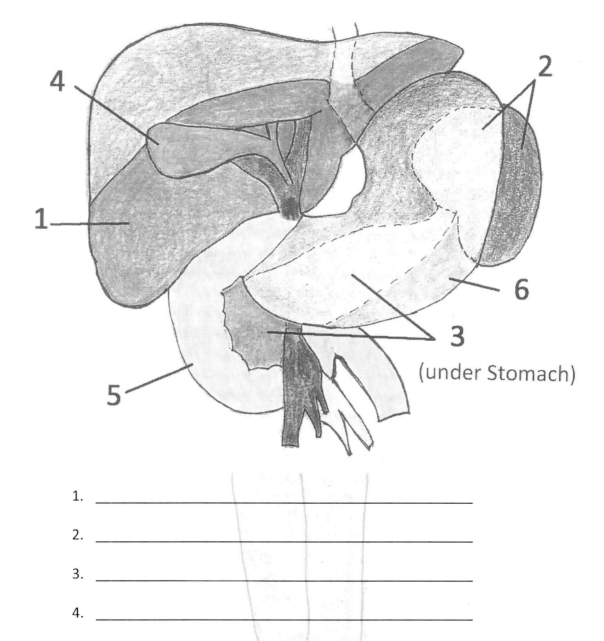

1. _____
2. _____
3. _____
4. _____
5. _____
6. _____

Investigation 3.6A/B   Dr._____

Crossword   Chronic Disease: Diabetes   P.____ Date:_____

Directions: Use the highlighted terms in the chapter to solve the puzzle. Most clues come from the chapter text, some require outside investigation. Omit spaces or dashes between words.

Medical Investigation 101 - Hill & Griffith

ACROSS

2 carbohydrates are broken to this; another name for sugar
7 the long, slender organ behind and below the stomach that produces insulin and glucagon
11 the food group that includes butter, lard, and cream
12 the care provided by family pratitioners who triage and treat or refer patient
13 carrying more weight than is healthy; a leading indicator of diabetic risk
16 the carpenter of medical doctors who treats mainly bones and joints with surgery
19 sending a patient to another physician or medical support team member for expertise or service
20 extreme or deep knowledge on a subject
21 the type of diabetes where the patient is making insulin but their cells don't absorb glucose properly
22 the surgery calendar at each hospital that tells surgeons when it is their turn to operate on their patient

DOWN

1 a visit to an orthopedist to evaluate a bone or joint problem and discover how it can best be treated
3 treatment with medicines and exercises; non-surgical treatments
4 a treatment plan; the treatments ordered by the physician to hopefully solve the problem
5 a diet recommended for diabetic patients where they ear few carbohydrates, such as the Adkins Diet
6 an artificial joint or body part that replaces a worn out or missing part; a few examples are leg, knee, hand, eye
8 a test that was used years ago to diagnose diabetes. today we use the hemoglobin A1C test
9 the rapidly digested food group that includes rice, potatoes, pasta, bread, candybars, and cake
10 other physicians you might collaborate with
12 the food group that includes meats, poultry, fish, beans, lentils, and nuts
14 a hormone produced in the pancreas that lowers blood sugar
15 a test that measures the average blood sugar over the past two to three months
17 a disease related to the inability to breakdown carbohydrates
18 to give off, expel, release, push out

147

Investigation 3.7A

Dr. _____

Shoulder Pain

P._____ Date_____

Vocabulary 1: Definitions

Directions: Use the text, a dictionary, or the internet to write a definition for each term.

1. precipitate: _____
   _____

2. anti-inflammatory: _____
   _____

3. modalities: _____
   _____

4. pain scale: _____
   _____

5. cyst: _____
   _____

6. hypertension: _____
   _____

7. osseous: _____
   _____

8. mobilization: _____
   _____

9. crepitus: _____
   _____

10. splinting: _____
    _____

11. edema: _____
    _____

12. erythema: _____
    _____

Investigation 3.7A Dr. _____

Shoulder Pain P._____ Date_____

Vocabulary 2: Matching

Directions: Match the definitions on the right to the medical terms on the left.

1. _____ precipitate
2. _____ anti-inflammatory
3. _____ modalities
4. _____ pain scale
5. _____ cyst
6. _____ hypertension
7. _____ osseous
8. _____ mobilization
9. _____ crepitus
10. _____ splinting
11. _____ edema
12. _____ erythema

a. making a joint move or moveable
b. swelling of an area of tissue or around a joint
c. a rating scale describing the degree of pain felt
d. elevated blood pressure
e. medicine that stops or prevents inflammation
f. anything that causes something else to happen
g. redness of tissue overlying and area of inflammation or infection
h. available treatments for an illness or injury
i. tightening surrounding muscles to not moving an area to prevent pain and protect the injured area
j. grating sensation or sound from movement of severely arthritic joints
k. pertaining to bone
l. abnormal membrane-bordered sac containing semi-liquid material

Investigation 3.7A Dr. _____

Shoulder Pain P._____ Date_____

Vocabulary 3: Sentences

Directions: Write a sentence using each vocabulary term.

1. precipitate: _____
_____

2. anti-inflammatory:_____
_____

3. modalities: _____
_____

4. pain scale: _____
_____

5. cyst: _____
_____

6. hypertension: _____
_____

7. osseous: _____
_____

8. mobilization: _____
_____

9. crepitus: _____
_____

10. splinting: _____
_____

11. edema: _____
_____

12. erythema: _____
_____

Investigation 3.7A: Shoulder Pain Dr._____

Worksheet 2: Orthopedics, page 1   P.____Date:_____

Orthopedic Worksheet

1. Would you consider referring George to another physician to treat his shoulder?

    Yes   No

2. If yes, to which physician specialist would you refer George?

    _____

3. If you decided to continue this patient under your care for the immediate future, to which part of the physician support team might you refer George?

    _____

4. Assuming you referred your patient to an Orthopedist having sub-specialty training, which specialist would best serve this patient's needs?

    _____

5. Perhaps your interest in medicine leans more toward healing injuries than curing illness? Take this opportunity to research the training time required to enter the field of Orthopedic Surgery.

    a. Number of years undergraduate college education = _____

    b. Number of years of medical school education = _____

    c. Number of years Orthopedic Residency Training = _____

    d. Total number of years of college + medical training = _____

    e. Can an orthopedist become a sub-specialist with additional training?   Circle your answer: No, that's it.   or Yes

6. List and define three classifications of injury based on duration of symptoms:

    A. _____

    B. _____

    C. _____

Investigation 3.7A: Shoulder Pain   Dr._____

Worksheet 2, Orthopedics page 2

7. List ten surgical procedures performed by Orthopedic Surgeons.

   a. _____
   b. _____
   c. _____
   d. _____
   e. _____
   f. _____
   g. _____
   h. _____
   i. _____
   j. _____

8. List four types of non-surgical treatment provided by Orthopedists.

   a. _____
   b. _____
   c. _____
   d. _____

9. Name and describe two serious injuries commonly suffered by baseball pitchers.

   a. _____
      _____
   b. _____
      _____

10. Name two reasons an Orthopedic Surgeon might decide to operate on a patient.

    a. _____
    b. _____

Investigation 3.7A

Crossword 3.7A   **Shoulder Pain**

Directions: Use the highlighted terms in the chapter to solve the puzzle. Most clues come from the chapter text, some require outside investigation. Omit spaces or dashes between words.

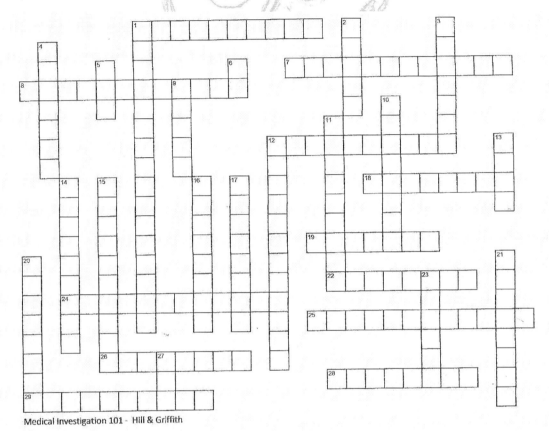

Medical Investigation 101 - Hill & Griffith

ACROSS

1. medical term meaning 'affecting' or causing pain or suffering
7. the medical name for high blood pressure
8. medical word for 'caused by'
12. therapeutic methods to treat a disease or injury; examples are surgery or chemotherapy
18. a grinding sensation caused by friction of bone rubbing against bone
19. located to the outside of midline
22. redness of the skin from inflammation
24. occurring on an irregular, non-continuous pattern
25. inflammation or infection of the appendix
26. the physical or mental clues caused by a disease
28. medical term for equal on both sides of the body
29. type of test used to evaluate muscle strength and symmetry

DOWN

1. a medicine that stops inflammation
2. swelling around a joint, such as occurs with a sprained ankle
3. referring to bone
4. an injury that occurred months or years ago that still causes pain or disability
5. medical abbreviation for 'twice a day'
6. medical abbreviation for 'once a day'
9. an injury that occurred in the last few days
10. referring to the front
11. the method doctors use to ask patients how bad it hurts; example: from 1 to 10
12. a type of activity designed to move a joint
13. an abnormal growth having a fluid-containing cavity
14. referring to the back
15. measurable factors or limits
16. an injury that occurred a week or two ago that still causes pain or disability
17. a condition where the body cannot process sugar adequately causing elevated levels of glucose in the blood
20. referring to the top
21. the hand you are more skilled at performing tasks
23. to cause a reaction
27. medical abbreviation for 'as needed'

Investigation 3.7B

Dr. _____

Joints

P. _____ Date _____

Vocabulary 1: Definitions

Directions: Use the text, a dictionary, or the internet to write a definition for each term.

1. ball and socket: _____
   _____

2. hinge: _____
   _____

3. flexion: _____
   _____

4. extension: _____
   _____

5. ligament: _____
   _____

6. muscles: _____
   _____

7. fusion: _____
   _____

8. joint: _____
   _____

9. synovial fluid: _____
   _____

10. articulating cartilage: _____
    _____

11. osteoarthritis: _____
    _____

12. rheumatoid arthritis: _____
    _____

Investigation 3.7B

Joints

Vocabulary 2: Matching

Dr. _____

P. _____ Date _____

Directions: Match the definitions at the right to the medical terms on the left.

1. _____ ball and socket
2. _____ hinge
3. _____ flexion
4. _____ extension
5. _____ ligament
6. _____ muscles
7. _____ fusion
8. _____ joint
9. _____ synovial fluid
10. _____ articulating cartilage
11. _____ osteoarthritis
12. _____ rheumatoid arthritis

a. joint allowing multi-directional movement and rotation
b. lubricating liquid material that assists smooth movement of joints
c. any place where two bones meet, regardless of the type of motion allowed
d. straightening of a joint, such as your elbow
e. when two osseous surfaces join to together such that no movement occurs
f. chronic progressive disease causing joint inflammation, pain, and immobility
g. tissues providing the power to move joints, attached to bones by tendons
h. bending a joint, such as your knee
i. the white, smooth surface of a normal joint where two bones are joined
j. the type of joint that moves like a door, such as your elbow
k. destruction of a joint due to wear and tear over several years
l. structures that connect bone to bone

Investigation 3.7B

Joints

Dr. _____

P._____ Date _____

Vocabulary 3: Sentences

Directions: Use each term below in a sentence.

1. ball and socket: _____

2. hinge: _____

3. flexion: _____

4. extension: _____

5. ligament: _____

6. muscles: _____

7. fusion: _____

8. joint: _____

9. synovial fluid: _____

10. articulating cartilage: _____

11. osteoarthritis: _____

12. rheumatoid arthritis: _____

Investigation 3.7B: Joints   Dr._____

Worksheet 1: Joints   Per: ____ Date:_____

Joints Worksheet

Directions: Answer the following questions about joints. You may refer to your previous reading in this section.

1. What is a joint? _____

2. Name three types of joints according to their degree and range of motion.

    a. _____

    b. _____

    c. _____

3. Describe the action of a ball and socket joint. _____
   _____

4. Give an example of a ball and socket joint in humans. _____

5. Provide a non-human example of a ball and socket joint. _____

6. Describe the action of a hinge joint. _____
   _____

7. Provide an example of a hinge joint found on the human body.
   _____

8. Think of a non-human hinge joint and write it below.
   _____

9. Provide an example of slightly moveable joints in humans. _____

10. What structure encompasses (encloses) a joint? _____

11. What connects the bones across a joint? _____

12. What structure powers bones and joints to move? _____

13. Name two structures that allow smooth movement of a joint and protect it from wearing out:

    a. _____   b. _____

Investigation 3.7B: Joints   Dr._____

Worksheet 1: Joints, page 2

14. Give an example of slightly moveable joints in your body.
_____

15. What disease occurs in older people when the smooth sliding surfaces of their joints wear out? _____

16. What disease occurs in young and older people where their immune system attacks joints within their own body? _____

17. Place your dominant hand on top of your head touching the top of your ear on the other side. Keep it there for five minutes by the clock while you straighten up your room or help out in the kitchen. Write a paragraph about your experience not having the use of your arm. What simple things could you no longer do?

_____
_____
_____
_____
_____
_____
_____
_____
_____
_____
_____
_____
_____
_____

Investigation 3.7B Dr._____

Crossword 3.7B **Joints** P.____Date:_____

Directions: Use the highlighted terms in the chapter to solve the puzzle. Most clues come from the chapter text, some require outside investigation. Omit spaces or dashes between words.

Mediccal Investigation 101 - Hill & Griffith

ACROSS

4 the thick liquid inside the joint capsule that lubricates the joint
5 the bones that surround and protect the brain
7 soft tissue structures holding connecting bone to bone; create leverage to perform work
8 a place in your body where minimal motion is desired at joints
15 the protective surface of bone that works with the opposing bone of a joint within the capsule
17 where all normal movement occurs in our body
18 provides the power to flex the forearm at the elbow
19 joints capable of movement and motion through a range of motions and directions
20 the condition where joint degeneration has occurred

DOWN

1 an autoimmune disease where joints become inflamed and destroyed; often bilaterally symmetrical pattern of destruction
2 supply the power to create movement
3 the joining together of certain bones at the end of growth
6 moving an object using a pivot point
9 the joint motion occurring when you stand from a sitting position
10 supplies the power to straighten your arm from a flexed position
11 the joint motion when you lift a glass of water to take a drink
12 joints moving along one axis in either flexion or extension
13 the process of bone growth and development
14 the breaking down of the cartilage surface of bone in a joint
16 the tissue that surrounds and encloses a joint

159

Investigation 3.8A   Dr. _____

Fever and Cough   P._____ Date_____

Vocabulary 1: Definitions

Directions: Use the text, a dictionary, or the internet to write a definition for each term.

1. viral infection: _____
   _____

2. mononucleosis: _____
   _____

3. measles: _____
   _____

4. chicken pox: _____
   _____

5. lymph nodes: _____
   _____

6. thyroid gland: _____
   _____

7. rhonchi: _____
   _____

8. sputum: _____
   _____

9. bowel sounds: _____
   _____

10. genetic disease: _____
    _____

11. infectious disease: _____
    _____

12. malignancy: _____
    _____

Investigation 3.8A　　　　　　　　　　　　　　　Dr. _____

Fever and Cough　　　　　　　　　　　　　　　P._____Date_____

Vocabulary 2: Matching

Directions: Match the definitions on the right to the medical terms on the left.

1. _____ viral infection
2. _____ mononucleosis
3. _____ measles
4. _____ chicken pox
5. _____ lymph nodes
6. _____ thyroid gland
7. _____ rhonchi
8. _____ sputum
9. _____ bowel sounds
10. _____ genetic disease
11. _____ infectious disease
12. _____ malignancy

a. a mixture of saliva and mucous from the respiratory tract
b. children viral illness that can reappear years later as shingles
c. illness caused by bacteria, viruses, fungi, or parasites
d. infection caused by a virus, such as influenza or zika
e. small bodies along lymphatic system that filter bacteria as part of our immune system
f. a disorder caused by abnormal gene(s) inherited from one or both parents
g. rattling, low pitch sounds emanating from the lungs
h. infectious childhood viral disease causing skin rash
i. normal sounds from abdomen caused by peristalsis
j. the presence of cancer
k. known as kissing disease, a viral illness spread in saliva
l. gland in neck producing hormones affecting metabolic rate

Investigation 3.8A

Fever and Cough

Vocabulary 3: Sentences

Dr. _____

P. _____ Date _____

Directions: Use each term in a complete sentence.

1. viral infection: _____
   _____

2. mononucleosis: _____
   _____

3. measles: _____
   _____

4. chicken pox: _____
   _____

5. lymph nodes: _____
   _____

6. thyroid gland: _____
   _____

7. rhonchi: _____
   _____

8. sputum: _____
   _____

9. bowel sounds: _____
   _____

10. genetic disease: _____
    _____

11. infectious disease: _____
    _____

12. malignancy: _____
    _____

Investigation 3.8A: Fever & Cough Dr._____

Worksheet : Fever & Cough P.____ Date:_____

Fever & Cough

Patient Name: _____ Age: _____ Gender: _____

Wt: _____ lbs.   Respirations: _____/min   Pulse: _____/min

Blood Pressure: _____/_____ mmHg   Temperature: _____ F.

CC: _____

HxCC: (List important information from the patient in your history of the chief complaint)

1. _____
2. _____
3. _____
4. _____
5. _____
6. _____
7. _____
8. _____

ROS: (List all positive findings from Review of Systems)-

1. _____
2. _____
3. _____
4. _____
5. _____

Positive Examination Findings:

1. _____
2. _____
3. _____
4. _____

Investigation 3.8A: Fever & Cough   Dr._____

Workup, Page 2

DDX: (List your three most likely diagnoses from the Diagnosis Grid)

1. _____
2. _____
3. _____

DDX-2: List the disorders from your DDX list you **ruled out** immediately because their symptoms did not fit this patient's history and physical exam findings:

1. _____
2. _____
3. _____

Put an X next to the tests you select first to investigate this patient's medical problem. Write <u>NA</u> for any test listed that is probably not appropriate to your evaluation of this condition:

- _____ X-rays of chest and lungs
- _____ Complete Blood Count (CBC)
- _____ MRI of the Chest
- _____ Ultrasound Study of chest
- _____ Culture and Sensitivity of Sputum
- _____ PPD test for TB

Lab Test Results:

Lab Test	Normal	Results
Chest X-Ray	Lungs clear; Immediate results	Positive for cavities in left lung
PPD	Results in 3 days; No reaction	Positive reaction; Redness at test site
Culture & Sensitivity of Sputum	Light diverse bacterial growth	Acid-Fast Bacilli smear and culture positive for (TB) Mycobacterium tuberculosis

Investigation 3.8A: Fever & Cough Dr._____

Workup Page 3 P.___Date:_____

Lab Test Summary: Record positive lab test findings from your lab tests (above):

1. _____
2. _____
3. _____

How do we know the lung cavities seen on the chest x-ray are in the left lung?

_____
_____
_____

Why was it important to take a Chest x-ray instead of waiting for the PPD test or the sputum culture?

_____
_____
_____

Your Diagnosis? (Hint: It is listed on the DDX list)

_____

Treatment Recommendations (Select type of treatment(s) you would recommend)

a. _____
b. _____
c. _____

Investigation 3.8A: Fever & Cough   Dr._____

Workup Page 4

Check the appropriate box to indicate how <u>Tuberculosis</u> spreads from one person to another (more than one method of spreading may exist):

TB Method of spreading	yes	no
• Breathing TB droplets in the air		
• Skin to skin contact with another person		
• Touching contaminated door handle		
• Sharing a glass		
• Contact with contaminated blood		
• Kissing a TB infected person		
• Contact with bedding or toilet seat		
• Cannot be spread to others		

Why do you think antibiotics have worked in the past to cure tuberculosis, but more recently may not work so well?

_____
_____
_____
_____

Reflections:

1. What was your patient's chief complaint? _____

2. Would you consider Manjula's complaint to be:

    (circle)   **Acute**   **Subacute**   or   **Chronic**

    a. Why?

    _____
    _____
    _____

Investigation 3.8A: Fever & Cough   Dr._____

Workup Page 5   P.___ Date:_____

3. How would you classify Manjula's condition (circle your answer)?

    Possible Emergency   or   Probably Non-Emergency

4. Why is Manjula's condition an emergency or non-emergency?

    _____
    _____

5. Which DDx possibilities did you **rule out** right away?

    a. _____
    b. _____
    c. _____

6. Is Tuberculosis caused by an **injury or illness**? (Circle your answer)

7. Is Tuberculosis preventable? How or why not?

    _____
    _____
    _____
    _____
    _____
    _____
    _____

8. Why is it important to diagnose and treat patients suspected of having Tuberculosis?

    _____
    _____
    _____

Investigation 3.8A Dr._____

Crossword 3.8A **Fever & Cough** P.____Date:_____

Directions: Use the highlighted terms in the chapter to solve the puzzle. Most clues come from the chapter text, some require outside investigation. Omit spaces or dashes between words.

ACROSS

1. a large gland in the neck that secretes hormones affecting our metabolism
5. relating to or affecting breathing
6. known as 'kissing disease'; caused by the Epstein-Barr virus
11. a rapid release of air from the lungs, often to remove irritants or mucus
14. the presence of cancerous tumors
16. a mixture of saliva and mucus resulting from infection or disease in respiratory tract
17. low pitched, rattling lung sounds that suggest mucus or obstruction of the respiratory tract
18. lung inflammation caused by bacterial or viral infection
19. cavities or spaces within bones or tissue, notably in the face or skull; examples are the nasal cavities

DOWN

2. the body's ability to fight off exposure to an infection or disease
3. the process by which living organisms change over time to assure survival
4. a malignant growth of abnormal cells
7. the way something looks or the proportion of its features
8. an infectious bacterial disease associated with growth of nodules in lungs; spread by coughing
9. an infectious disease caused by the herpes zoster virus; can re-emerge as shingles later in life
10. normal noises from the abdomen from muscular contractions of peristalsis
12. small, bean-shaped organs located along the lymphatic system that filter bacteria and foreign particles from lymph fluid
13. an infectious viral disease causing fever and a red rash; more common in childhood
15. cancer of the lymph nodes

Investigation 3.8B   Dr. _____

Pulmonary Embolism   P._____ Date_____

Vocabulary 1: Definitions

Directions: Use the text, a dictionary, or the internet to write a definition for each term.

1. respiratory system: _____
   _____

2. carbon dioxide: _____
   _____

3. oxygen: _____
   _____

4. diaphragm: _____
   _____

5. trachea: _____
   _____

6. epiglottis: _____
   _____

7. emphysema: _____
   _____

8. carcinogenic: _____
   _____

9. bronchi: _____
   _____

10. villi: _____
    _____

11. bronchioles: _____
    _____

12. alveoli: _____
    _____

Investigation 3.8B   Dr. _____

Pulmonary Embolism   P._____ Date_____

Vocabulary 2: Matching

Directions: Match the definitions on the right to the medical terms on the left.

1. _____ respiratory system
2. _____ carbon dioxide
3. _____ oxygen
4. _____ diaphragm
5. _____ trachea
6. _____ epiglottis
7. _____ emphysema
8. _____ carcinogenic
9. _____ bronchi
10. _____ villi
11. _____ bronchioles
12. _____ alveoli

a. The respiratory system air sacs where oxygen/carbon dioxide exchange occurs
b. Inhaled by humans, given off by plants
c. cartilaginous cover that keeps food out of our windpipe
d. hair-like structures in our respiratory tract that helps move mucous upward
e. the group of organs that allows us to breathe and exchange oxygen and carbon dioxide throughout the body
f. disorder where the lungs air sacs are damaged, common in smokers
g. dome-shaped muscle that contracts for inspiration and relaxes during exhalation
h. removed from the atmosphere by plants, exhaled by humans
i. the two main branches of the trachea heading toward the lungs
j. the windpipe; tube through which air moves to and from the lungs
k. anything thought to have the potential to cause cancer
l. the many tiny air tubes connecting the bronchi to the alveoli

Investigation 3.8B Dr. _____

Pulmonary Embolism P. _____ Date _____

Vocabulary 3: Sentences

Directions: Use each term in a complete sentence.

1. respiratory system: _____
   _____

2. carbon dioxide: _____
   _____

3. oxygen: _____
   _____

4. diaphragm: _____
   _____

5. trachea: _____
   _____

6. epiglottis: _____
   _____

7. emphysema: _____
   _____

8. carcinogenic: _____
   _____

9. bronchi: _____
   _____

10. villi: _____
    _____

11. bronchioles: _____
    _____

12. alveoli: _____
    _____

Investigation 3.8B: Respiratory System　　　　　　　　Dr. _____

Worksheet 3.8　　　　　　　　　　　　　　　　　　　P.___ Date:_____

Directions: Answer the questions based on your reading of 3.8B.

1. Air enters the respiratory system by way of the _____ and _____.

2. The two main ingredients in our air are _____ and _____.

3. _____ (a gas) makes up 78% of the air we breathe.

4. The _____ covers the trachea and protects the airway from food and liquids from the mouth.

5. The lungs are located in the _____.

6. Air travels to the lungs by moving through the _____ system.

7. Air enters the lungs by way of the _____.

8. From the bronchi the air then moves to the _____.

9. Oxygen is exchanged for carbon dioxide in the _____.

10. The lining covering the lungs is the _____.

11. What provides the energy for inspiration (breathing in)?

    _____

    _____

12. What happens to allow us to exhale air from our lungs?

    a. _____

    b. _____

13. Name three ways we might expose our lungs to a toxic environment.

    a. _____

    b. _____

    c. _____

Investigation 3.8B: Respiratory System   Dr._____

Worksheet 3.8B, page 2

14. Pretty much everyone who smokes for many years will end up suffering from _____.(disease)

15. What names have been given to those suffering from emphysema? _____ and _____

16. Many people who smoke for many years end up with what diseases?
_____
_____

17. Tar in cigarettes is considered a _____, which means it can cause cancer.

18. Children exposed to second hand smoke and other air-toxins can develop _____.

19. Which area of the lung is most destroyed by smoking? _____

20. What function do villi perform in our trachea?
_____
_____

Investigation 3.8B: Respiratory System   Dr._____

Worksheet 3.8.B, page 3   P.___Date:_____

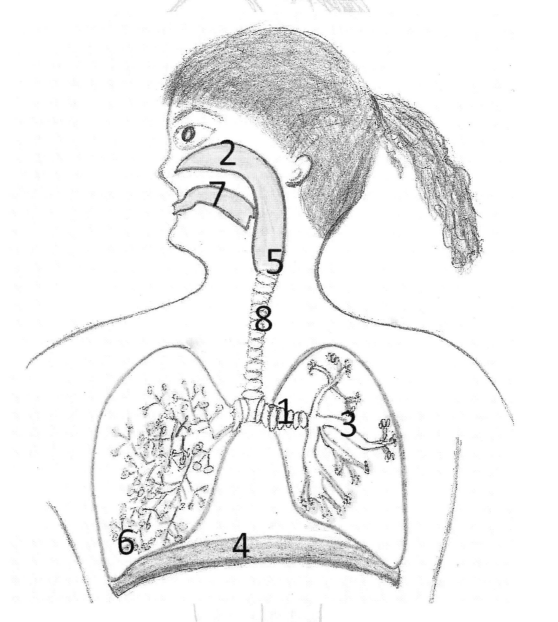

Directions: Write the names of the structures of the respiratory tract next to the number.

1._____ 5._____

2._____ 6._____

3._____ 7._____

4._____ 8._____

Investigation 3.8B Dr._____

Crossword 3.8B **Lungs** P.____Date:_____

Directions: Use the highlighted terms in the chapter to solve the puzzle. Most clues come from the chapter text, some require outside investigation. Omit spaces or dashes between words.

Medical Investigation 101 - Hill & Griffith

ACROSS

1. the outer covering of the lungs
3. the branches off of the bronchi
7. the system of organs allowing you to inhale, exhale, and exchange oxygen and carbon dioxide
9. the tiny air sacs in the lungs where exchange of oxygen and carbon dioxide take place
11. absorbed by plants and converted in photosynthesis to carbon and oxygen
14. tiny hair-like projections lining the trachea that help move mucous
15. capable of spreading from one person to another
17. nickname given those who suffer from emphysema
18. the major organs where oxygen and carbon dioxide exchange occurs
20. the two major branches of the trachea leading to the lungs
21. microscopic living organisms; only about 1% cause disease
24. anything that causes infection or disease
25. the process of taking in oxygen and releasing carbon dioxide; the action of breathing
26. one of the products of photosynthesis; carried by hemoglobin to cells throughout the body
27. the cartilaginous cover protecting the trachea from inhaling food
28. a condition where alveoli are damaged and enlarged, making it difficult to exhale air

DOWN

2. to breathe out; to release carbon dioxide
4. anything having the potential to cause cancer
5. the most major component of the air we breathe
6. inflammation of the bronchi
8. the chemical processes that help us maintain life; the rate at which our bodies use energy
10. molecules we inhale containing 78% nitrogen and 21% oxygen
12. lubricates the trachea and moves dust and other contaminants out of respiratory system
13. dome-shaped muscular wall separating the abdomen from the thorax; assists breathing; a spasm causes hiccups
16. organisms incapable of life without a host; use host DNA or RNA to reproduce
19. the area of the body between the neck and abdomen containing many important organs
22. the windpipe connecting the nose and mouth to the lungs
23. a parasitic infection spread throughout the world by mosquitos

Investigation 3.9A Dr. _____

Abdominal Pain & Dark Urine P.____ Date_____

Vocabulary 1: Definitions

Directions: Use the text, a dictionary, or the internet to write a definition for each term.

1. general anesthesia: _____
   _____

2. consultation: _____
   _____

3. immunizations: _____
   _____

4. hypertension: _____
   _____

5. hematuria: _____
   _____

6. blood urea nitrogen: _____
   _____

7. creatinine: _____
   _____

8. kidney filtration rate: _____
   _____

9. intravenous pyelogram: _____
   _____

10. bedside manner: _____
    _____

11. autosomal dominant: _____
    _____

12. polycystic kidney disease: _____
    _____

Investigation 3.9A Dr. _____

Abdominal Pain & Dark Urine P._____ Date _____

Vocabulary 2: Matching

Directions: Match the definitions on the right to the medical terms on the left.

1. _____ general anesthesia

2. _____ consultation

3. _____ immunizations

4. _____ hypertension

5. _____ hematuria

6. _____ blood urea nitrogen

7. _____ creatinine

8. _____ kidney filtration rate

9. _____ intravenous pyelogram

10. _____ bedside manner

11. _____ autosomal dominant

12. _____ polycystic kidney disease

a. a physician having special training examines another physician's patient
b. an ongoing condition of elevated blood pressure
c. test measuring the amount of nitrogen in the blood performed to determine how well the kidneys are functioning
d. the flow rate of filtered fluid through the kidneys
e. the doctor's approach or attitude towards his/her patients
f. a genetic disorder where abnormal cysts form and grow in the kidneys
g. an x-ray examination of the kidneys, ureters, and urinary bladder using injected iodinated contrast material
h. vaccinations that provide immunity to bacterial or viral diseases
i. inducing a state of unconsciousness with the absence of pain perception over the entire body
j. passing on a trait or disorder where the gene is expressed, even if carried by only one parent
k. a waste product of muscle metabolism filtered out by kidneys and eliminated in urine
l. the presence of blood in the urine; blood in the urine is always abnormal

Investigation 3.9A Dr. _____

Abdominal Pain & Dark Urine P.____Date_____

Vocabulary 3: Sentences

Directions: Write a sentence using each term.

1. general anesthesia: _____
   _____

2. consultation: _____
   _____

3. immunizations: _____
   _____

4. hypertension: _____
   _____

5. hematuria: _____
   _____

6. blood urea nitrogen: _____
   _____

7. creatinine: _____
   _____

8. kidney filtration rate: _____
   _____

9. intravenous pyelogram: _____
   _____

10. bedside manner: _____
    _____

11. autosomal dominant: _____
    _____

12. polycystic kidney disease: _____
    _____

Investigation 3.9A Dr._____

Worksheet 3.9A: Abdominal and Back Pain and Dark Urine P.____Date_____

Directions: Answer the following questions which are based on your reading of the preceding case study.

1. As the consulting physician in this case, which specialty of medicine do you most likely practice? _____

2. What may be America's greatest contribution to healthcare?
   _____

3. As the consulting physician on a patient you do not know, what is the first step in beginning to understand the reason you are examining the patient?
   _____

4. What medical issues are documented in the history and physical from Dr. Johnson?
   a. _____
   b. _____
   c. _____
   d. _____

5. What medication does Martha take each day? _____

6. What lab test result gave you a great deal of information?
   _____

7. What is the normal kidney filtration rate? _____

8. What was Martha's kidney filtration rate? _____

9. What are the two positive findings in your examination?
   _____
   _____

Investigation 3.9A – Abdominal and Back Pain and Dark Urine

Worksheet, Page 2 Dr._____

Disease	Nausea/ Vomit	Pain	Pain	Painful Urination	Fever/ Chills	Hematuria	Frequent Urination	Other
Urinary Infection	X	Upper back	side	X	X	X	X	acute
Pyelo-nephritis	X	Upper back	side	X	X		X	Acute or chronic
Kidney Stones	X	Sudden, severe abdominal				X		acute
Upper Urinary Tract Infection	X		side	X	X		X	acute
Cystitis		pelvic		X	X	X	X	Acute or chronic
Kidney Cancer		Low back or none	mass		X	X		Appetite loss
Polycystic Kidney Disease		abdominal	side	If kidney stones		X	X	Hyper-tension chronic
Leptso-spirosis	X	Headache, low back,	calf		X			Jaundice, appetite loss
Martha								

Add Martha's symptoms at the **bottom row** of the chart and compare them to the rest of the differential diagnosis list.

Investigation 3.9A

Worksheet 3.9, page 3

Dr._____

P.____Date_____

10. Which disease(s) do Martha's symptoms most match?
    _____

11. What is hematuria? _____

12. What is the purpose of Lisinopril? Treatment of _____

13. What potential problem can a IVP (intravenous pyelogram) cause that makes you hesitant to utilize this test?
    _____
    _____

14. What test did you order to evaluate Martha's kidneys? _____

15. What were the findings of the test ordered in #14?
    _____, _____ right & _____ left kidney

16. What do the test results confirm as your diagnosis?
    _____

17. Is this disease infectious or genetic? _____

18. Is this disease acute or chronic? _____

19. What are the 3 important functions of the kidneys?
    a. _____
    b. _____
    c. _____

20. Why would Martha take a blood pressure medicine when she has kidney disease?
    _____

21. Is Polycystic Kidney Disease a local disease or diffuse? _____

22. What other complications can occur in this disease?
    _____
    _____

Investigation 3.9A Dr._____

Worksheet 3.9, page 3

23. Why would it be important to advise Martha's children's pediatrician of her condition?
_____
_____

24. Is there a cure for Martha's illness? _____

25. Could Martha ever be a candidate for a kidney transplant? _____

26. Do you think it would be difficult to tell Martha about her illness? Why?
_____
_____
_____

Investigation 3.9A   Dr._____

Crossword   **Abdominal Pain**   P.____ Date:_____

Directions: Use the highlighted terms in the chapter to solve the puzzle. Most clues come from the chapter text, but some require outside investigation. Omit spaces or dashes between words.

Medical Investigation 101 - Hill & Griffith

ACROSS

1 an infection that starts in the urethra or bladder and travels up to the kidney
8 a place where surgical procedures are performed
14 one's chosen profession; how one earns money
15 a test to help diagnose kidney disease; acronym is BUN
16 organ responsible for filtering liquid waste from the blood
17 a physician who specializes in diseases of the kidney
24 the rate at which waste products are filtered from blood traveling through the kidneys
25 involving or showing violence or bloodshed
26 the specialty of medical practice dealing with prevention, diagnosis, and treatment of adult diseases
27 a physician who specializes in problems in the urinary tract
28 involved deeply in an activity or interest

DOWN

2 the medical record of each patient

3 control or manage
4 a calcium mass forming in the kidney; known to be very painful
5 vaccines stimulating the immune system to protect against infection or disease
6 a genetic disorder where numerous cysts grow in the kidneys
7 the people you work with
9 a fellow physician from whom you request advice or services based on their expertise
10 a chemical waste molecule resulting from muscle metabolism and excreted in urine; also tested to determine health of kidneys
11 medical term for high blood pressure
12 the system that includes the kidneys, ureters, bladder and urethra
13 inducing unconsciousness for the purpose of performing a surgical procedure
18 comatose; unawake
19 to prevent or make impossible
20 medical term for blood in the urine
21 signs provided by patients about what they are feeling or experiencing; clues to direct your medical investigation
22 an x-ray of your urinary tract
23 the sac in which urine collects for eventual excretion when you pee

Investigation 3.9B

Dr. _____

Urinary Tract

P.____Date_____

Vocabulary 1: Definitions

Directions: Use the text, a dictionary, or the internet to write a definition for each term.

1. urinary tract: _____
   _____

2. kidneys: _____
   _____

3. hormone: _____
   _____

4. renal: _____
   _____

5. nephrons: _____
   _____

6. sphincter: _____
   _____

7. micturition reflex: _____
   _____

8. sterile: _____
   _____

9. urinary bladder: _____
   _____

10. urethra: _____
    _____

11. ureter: _____
    _____

12. urinary catheter: _____
    _____

Investigation 3.9B

Urinary Tract

Vocabulary 2: Matching

Dr. _____

P.____Date_____

Directions: Match the definitions on the right to the medical terms on the left.

1. _____ urinary tract
2. _____ kidneys
3. _____ hormone
4. _____ renal
5. _____ nephrons
6. _____ sphincter
7. _____ micturition reflex
8. _____ sterile
9. _____ urinary bladder
10. _____ urethra
11. _____ ureter
12. _____ urinary catheter

a. The part of the kidney where waste products are filtered from blood and urine produced
b. the system of organs that filter waste from blood and produce, store, and discharge urine
c. relating to the kidneys
d. the duct that carries urine from the urinary bladder to the outside world
e. the absence of bacteria and other living microorganisms
f. the organs that filter waste from blood and produce urine
g. the ring of muscle that prevents constant flow of urine
h. a tube inserted through the urethra into the urinary bladder to allow urine to drain
i. the hollow organ that collects and stores urine until it exits through the urethra
j. chemical produced in a gland that controls the function of other glands or organs
k. tube that sends urine from the kidneys to the urinary bladder
l. the signal telling you it's time to pee; occurs in response to increased bladder pressure

Investigation 3.9B

Urinary Tract

Vocabulary 3: Sentences

Dr. _____

P. _____ Date _____

Directions: Use each term in a sentence.

1. urinary tract: _____
   _____

2. kidneys: _____
   _____

3. hormone: _____
   _____

4. renal: _____
   _____

5. nephrons: _____
   _____

6. sphincter: _____
   _____

7. micturition reflex: _____
   _____

8. sterile: _____
   _____

9. urinary bladder: _____
   _____

10. urethra: _____
    _____

11. ureter: _____
    _____

12. urinary catheter: _____
    _____

Investigation 3.9B

Worksheet 3.9B: Urinary Tract

Dr._____

P.____Date:_____

1. What are the four main parts of the urinary tract?

    a. _____

    b. _____

    c. _____

    d. _____

2. What does 'renal' refer to? _____

3. How many kidneys do normal babies have at birth?_____

4. How does blood enter and leave the kidneys?

    Enters Kidneys: _____

    Leaves Kidneys: _____

5. What percent of material that filters through the kidneys returns to the blood?

    _____%

6. What do we call the little tubes inside the kidneys that do the complex filtering process?

    _____

7. About how many quarts of filtrate pass through the tubules of the kidneys per day?

    a. _____quarts/day

8. Approximately how much urine is produced every day? _____quarts/day

9. How much water do doctors recommend we drink each day to keep our kidneys filtering efficiently? _____ glasses

Worksheet 3.9B – Urinary Tract　　　　　　　　　　　　　　　Dr._____

Page 2

10. Through what structure must urine travel to get from the kidney to the bladder?

    _____

11. What causes urine to move from the kidneys to the bladder?

    a. _____

    b. _____

12. What is the purpose of the bladder?

    _____

    _____

13. Which reflex lets us know that it is time to urinate?

    _____

14. What acts as a facet to start and stop the flow of urine?

    _____

15. How does urine get from the bladder to the outside world?

    _____

16. Is urine sterile?   YES   NO   (circle your answer)

17. What is the main ingredient in urine? _____

18. Why do you think there is so much nitrogen present in urine?

    _____

    _____

Urinary Tract Worksheet – Diagram

Worksheet 3.9B

Dr._____

P.____Date:_____

Directions: Identify the parts of the urinary system and write their names on the line of the corresponding number.

Urinary Tract

1._____

2._____

3._____

4._____

5._____

6._____

7._____

8._____

9._____

Investigation 3.9B

Crossword 3.9B Urinary Tract

Directions: Use the highlighted terms in the chapter to solve the puzzle. Most clues come from the chapter text, some require outside investigation. Omit spaces or dashes between words.

Medical Investigation 101 - Hill & Griffith

ACROSS

3 these organs filter liquid waste from the blood
4 to become narrow or closed off
7 the absence of bacteria
8 a kidney tissue sample taken to diagnose disease or infection
9 makes up 78% of air; present in large amounts in urine
12 watery, yellowish fluid stored in bladder until discharged through the urethra
13 moves waste from the kidneys
14 a regulating chemical that stimulates specific cells into action
16 a condition of impaired kidney function where kidneys inadequately filter waste from the blood
17 the bag attached to the urinary catheter to collect urine output
18 the sytem that includes the kidneys, ureters, bladder, and urethra
19 tubes that move urine from the kidneys to the bladder
20 the basic filtering unit of the kidneys
21 place where urine is stored until you pee

DOWN

1 relaxation of the urethral sphincter in response to increased pressure in the bladder
2 a measurement of the systolic and diastolic arterial pressures
5 a ring of muscle surrounding an opening or tube serving to close off the tube; one example is located in the urethra
6 referring to the kidneys
8 supplies oxygen rich blood to the kidneys
10 a hollow tube inserted into urethra and bladder to collect urine in patients who cannot control their bladder
11 the act of urinating
15 tube that moves urine out of the bladder

Investigation 3.10A   Dr. _____

Weak & Dizzy   P._____ Date_____

Vocabulary 1: Definitions

Directions: Use the text, a dictionary, or the internet to write a definition for each term.

1. lymph nodes: _____
   _____

2. palpation: _____
   _____

3. liver: _____
   _____

4. hyperpigmentation: _____
   _____

5. estrogen: _____
   _____

6. pneumonia: _____
   _____

7. shingles: _____
   _____

8. tetanus booster: _____
   _____

9. Mees' lines: _____
   _____

10. arsenic: _____
    _____

11. metabolize: _____
    _____

12. excreted: _____
    _____

Investigation 3.10A

Weak and Dizzy

Vocabulary 2: Matching

Dr. _____

P._____Date_____

Directions: Match the definitions on the right to the medical terms on the left.

1. _____ lymph nodes
2. _____ palpation
3. _____ liver
4. _____ hyperpigmentation
5. _____ estrogen
6. _____ pneumonia
7. _____ shingles
8. _____ tetanus booster
9. _____ Mee's lines
10. _____ arsenic
11. _____ metabolize
12. _____ excreted

a. Large, glandular organ located in left upper quadrant, makes bile and involved in many metabolic processes
b. using the hands to examine the body while diagnosing illness
c. breaking down food into a form usable by your body
d. vaccine given during childhood and then every ten years thereafter to stimulate immunity to tetanus
e. hormones that promote the development of female characteristics
f. small bodies along lymphatic system that filter bacteria
g. discharged or given off as waste matter, such as carbon dioxide, urine, sweat, & feces
h. horizontal white lines across finger and toenails representing exposure to arsenic
i. acute inflammation along a nerve with skin rash caused by recurrence of chicken pox virus
j. darkening of an area of skin or nails caused by increased melanin
k. lung inflammation caused by bacterial or viral infection
l. element #33, a poison commonly found in insecticides and rat poisons, causes Mee's lines

Investigation 3.10A

Weak & Dizzy

Vocabulary 3: Sentences

Dr. _____

P. _____ Date _____

Directions: Use each term in a sentence.

1. lymph nodes: _____
   _____

2. palpation: _____
   _____

3. liver: _____
   _____

4. hyperpigmentation: _____
   _____

5. estrogen: _____
   _____

6. pneumonia: _____
   _____

7. shingles: _____
   _____

8. tetanus booster: _____
   _____

9. Mees' lines: _____
   _____

10. arsenic: _____
    _____

11. metabolize: _____
    _____

12. excreted: _____
    _____

Investigation 3.10A: Weak & Dizzy
Worksheet 3.10A,   page 1

Dr._____
P.____Date:_____

Directions: Refer to Investigation 3.10A to answer the following questions.

1. List Dorothy's symptoms that something is affecting her health:

    a. _____
    b. _____
    c. _____
    d. _____
    e. _____
    f. _____

2. What objective findings did you see in her physical examination?

    a. _____
    b. _____
    c. _____
    d. _____
    e. _____
    f. _____
    g. _____

3. Which laboratory tests did you order on Dorothy's first visit?

    a. _____
    b. _____
    c. _____
    d. _____
    e. _____

Investigation 3.10A: Weak & Dizzy Dr._____
Worksheet 3.10A   - page 2

4. What new symptoms did you observe at the second meeting with this patient?
   a. _____
   b. _____
   c. _____

5. What is the significance of Mee's Lines?
   _____
   _____

6. Which parts of the body are primarily affected in arsenic toxicity?
   a. _____
   b. _____
   c. _____
   d. _____
   e. _____

7. Where in the body is arsenic deposited that can easily be utilized to make a definitive diagnosis of arsenic toxicity?
   _____

8. What signs did Dorothy demonstrate that could indicate early pulmonary damage?
   _____

9. How can chronic arsenic exposure cause bladder cancer
   _____
   _____

10. What potential danger exists from buying fruits and vegetables imported from other countries?
    _____
    _____

11. Which medical laboratory test from the earlier list would you order to confirm your diagnosis of heavy metal poisoning with arsenic?
    _____

Investigation 3.10A Dr._____

Crossword 3.10A   **Weak & Dizzy**   P.____ Date:_____

Directions: Use the highlighted terms in the chapter to solve the puzzle. Most clues come from the chapter text, some require outside investigation. Omit spaces or dashes between words.

ACROSS

1. removed from the body: sweat, pee, or pooh
3. means best or greatest value
7. a specialist treating only disorders of the intestinal tract
11. small bodies located along the lymphatic system of the neck, armpits, and groin that filter bacteria and foreign particles from lymph fluid
14. deficiency of hemoglobin or red blood cells resulting in fatigue and pallor
15. yellowing of the whites of the eyes; occurs with jaundice of the liver
20. means white lines across the nail; Mees' lines sign of arsenic poisoning
22. large glandular organ in right upper quadrant having many metabolic functions
23. a poisonous element used in rat poison; causes Mees' lines in humans
25. organs responsible for filtering liquid waste from blood
26. female hormone; promotes female characteristics
27. related to the lungs or breathing
28. preventive innoculations used to confer immunity to specific diseases

5. changing food or medicine into a form useable or excreted by the body; performed by kidneys and liver
6. organ storing urine until you feel the urge to pee
8. periodic vaccination to prevent tetanus; after three doses immunity is usually achieved
9. the organ of the intestinal tract where food is stored and prepared for digestion
10. a list of all possible causes of an illness
12. condition where the skin darkens, from small areas to entire body
13. excess water loss caused by excess sweating, vomiting, or diarrhea
16. a method of bonding metallic ions, such as arsenic, for removal from the body
17. the area between the stomach and anus where food is digested and nutrients absorbed
18. not paying attention
19. to examine the patient by touch; example is palpating the liver
21. a physician treating only certain conditions or body systems
24. re-emergence of the virus years after chicken pox

DOWN

2. condition of liquid poop that can cause dehydration
4. bacterial or viral infection of the lungs

Investigation 3.10B

Dr. _____

Environmental Toxins

P._____ Date_____

Vocabulary 1: Definitions

Directions: Use the text, a dictionary, or the internet to write a definition for each term.

1. toxins: _____
   _____

2. debilitating: _____
   _____

3. lead: _____
   _____

4. cadmium: _____
   _____

5. mercury: _____
   _____

6. radioactive: _____
   _____

7. PCB's: _____
   _____

8. pesticides: _____
   _____

9. prescription drugs: _____
   _____

10. World Health Organization: _____
    _____

11. carcinogenic: _____
    _____

12. chronic exposure: _____
    _____

Investigation 3.10B

Environmental Toxins

Vocabulary 2: Matching

Dr. _____

P. _____ Date _____

Directions: Match the definitions on the right to the terms on the left.

1. _____ toxins
2. _____ debilitating
3. _____ lead
4. _____ cadmium
5. _____ mercury
6. _____ radioactive
7. _____ PCB's
8. _____ pesticides
9. _____ prescription drugs
10. _____ World Health Organization
11. _____ carcinogenic
12. _____ chronic exposure

a. chemicals used to kill pests that also get into our water and land
b. repeated contact over a protracted period of time
c. metal used in chrome rims and rechargeable batteries, toxic to humans
d. agency of the United Nations concerned with international public health
e. a disease or condition that makes someone very weak and unhealthy
f. toxic compounds used in the manufacture of plastics
g. potentially capable of causing cancer
h. chemicals prescribed by physicians affecting the human body in negative ways when misused
i. element #80, a toxic metal used at one time in thermometers, batteries, florescent lights, and more
j. having or producing powerful and dangerous radiation; overexposure linked to cancer
k. atomic number 82, Pb has been used in water carrying pipes, especially toxic to children
l. poisonous substances capable of causing health problems

Investigation 3.10B Dr. _____

Environmental Toxins P. _____ Date _____

Vocabulary 3: Sentences

Directions: Use each term in a sentence.

1. toxins: _____
   _____

2. debilitating: _____
   _____

3. lead: _____
   _____

4. cadmium: _____
   _____

5. mercury: _____
   _____

6. radioactive: _____
   _____

7. PCB's: _____
   _____

8. pesticides: _____
   _____

9. prescription drugs: _____
   _____

10. World Health Organization: _____
    _____

11. carcinogenic: _____
    _____

12. chronic exposure: _____
    _____

Investigation 3.10B Dr._____

Worksheet 3.10B P.___ Date:_____

Environmental Toxins

Directions: Answer the following questions based on your reading of investigation 3.10B, Environmental Toxins.

1. What international organization tracks environmental toxins around the world?
   _____

2. Potential sources of environmental toxins, even here in the U.S., can be found in:

    a. _____
    b. _____
    c. _____
    d. _____
    e. _____

3. Which toxin does Pure Earth continue to rate as the leading debilitating toxin in the entire world?
   _____

4. Which heavy metal toxin, also associated with the processing of car batteries, has poisoned U.S. citizens' water supply and was once found in paint?
   _____

5. Which heavy metal affected first responders to the World Trade Center terrorist attack?
   _____

6. Formerly used in thermometers, construction, florescent lights, and many other things, this heavy metal has spread into our lakes and oceans and into our fish supply, including tuna, swordfish, shark and King mackerel. This heavy metal is:_____

7. Our government's testing of nuclear materials and building of nuclear power plants has exposed our citizens to the potential of poisoning by which heavy metal?
   _____

Investigation 3.10B Dr._____

Worksheet 3.10B, page 2

8. Which two countries experienced very serious nuclear disasters related to the operation of their nuclear power plants?

    a. _____

    b. _____

9. Which pesticide was used extensively to control mosquitos and pests attacked crops until 1972, yet still contaminates our air, water, and soil?

    _____

10. What have the burning fossil fuels in our cars, trucks, trains, planes, and factories worldwide spewed into our air that scientists feel has raised the CO_2 level of our atmosphere and caused climate change?

    c. _____

    d. _____

11. About how many people does the World Health Organization estimate die each year as a direct result of air pollution?

    _____

12. Why does most exposure to toxic chemicals occur inside the home?

    _____
    _____
    _____

13. Write a paragraph explaining your thoughts about the greatest environmental concerns for the area where you live.

    _____
    _____
    _____
    _____
    _____
    _____
    _____

Investigation 3.10B Dr._____

Crossword 3.10B   **Environmental Toxins**   P.____ Date:_____

Directions: Use the highlighted terms in the chapter to solve the puzzle. Most clues come from the chapter text, but some require outside investigation. Omit spaces or dashes between words.

Medical Investigation 101 - Hill & Griffith

ACROSS

4 toxic chemical contaminating ocean fish; no longer used in thermometers
5 Russian city famous for nuclear power plant disaster in 1986
8 disorders producing signs or symptoms and not the result of injury
10 the place where you live, including the air, your food and water, even your home
11 a natural radioactive material that seeps upward from within Earth; sometimes present in igneous rock, soil, and water
13 clean, safe living conditions
15 pertaining to the nervous system, including the brain, spinal cord, or nerves
16 country that suffered nuclear disaster in 2011 following an earthquake and tsunami
18 a known neurotoxin causing permanent brain and nerve damage; the cause of poisoning of children in Flint, Michigan
19 ends up as second hand smoke; a known carcinogen
20 things in our environment that can impair our health
21 radioactive material used in nuclear bombs
22 toxic metal used in making chrome wheels; was the main toxin in World Trade Center attack in 2001
23 form of plastic banned in 1976 because of its toxicity to health
24 how undetected toxins cause cancer and other serious diseases

DOWN

1 when toxic things are introduced into our environment; example, water seeps into our drinking water
2 the group that estimates 4.6 million people die each year from air pollution
3 the chief doctor of the United States; at one time actually promoted smoking as a healthy lifestyle
6 emitting of ionizing radiation or particles; capable of producing a powerful and dangerous form of energy
7 discarding these down the toilet spreads them to the water system, causing mutations in animals and fish
9 causing illness or disability from exposure
12 any chemical that causes cancer
14 known as fragrance plastics; used in shower curtains and toys
17 chemicals used to eradicate mosquitos and other pests; also toxic to humans

Investigation 3.11A

Dr. _____

Food-borne Illness

P. _____ Date _____

Vocabulary 1: Definitions

Directions: Use the text, a dictionary, or the internet to write a definition for each term.

1. Food-borne illness: _____
   _____

2. CDC: _____
   _____

3. pathogens: _____
   _____

4. inoculate: _____
   _____

5. stools: _____
   _____

6. culture: _____
   _____

7. antitoxin: _____
   _____

8. salmonella: _____
   _____

9. norovirus: _____
   _____

10. toxoplasmosis: _____
    _____

11. Department of Health: _____
    _____

12. food preparation guidelines: _____
    _____

Investigation 3.11A

Food-borne Illness

Vocabulary 2: Matching

Dr. _____

P. _____ Date _____

Directions: Match the definitions on the right to the terms on the left.

1. _____ food-borne illness
2. _____ CDC
3. _____ pathogens
4. _____ inoculate
5. _____ stools
6. _____ culture
7. _____ antitoxin
8. _____ salmonella
9. _____ norovirus
10. _____ toxoplasmosis
11. _____ Department of Health
12. _____ food preparation guidelines

a. common foodborne pathogen causing 'stomach flu'; strikes quickly but typically resolves in 2-3 days
b. growing of pathogens in lab to determine organism and sensitivity
c. a bacteria, virus, or other microorganism capable of causing disease
d. food poisoning; illness resulting from eating food contaminated by pathogens or chemical toxins
e. safe steps for food preparation, handling, storage, and cooking
f. parasitic infection transmitted through undercooked meat, or from soil or cat feces
g. an antibody capable of neutralizing a specific toxin
h. acronym for Centers for Disease Control & Prevention whose goal is improving public health
i. introducing a toxic agent or a helpful vaccine into an organism
j. the place where foodborne illness is reported by physicians
k. gram-negative rod-shaped bacteria that causes food-borne illness by fecal contamination of food or water
l. human feces; poop

Investigation 3.11A

Food-borne Illness

Vocabulary 3: Sentences

Dr. _____

P._____ Date _____

Directions: Use each term in a sentence.

1. Food-borne illness: _____
   _____

2. CDC: _____
   _____

3. pathogens: _____
   _____

4. inoculate: _____
   _____

5. stools: _____
   _____

6. culture: _____
   _____

7. antitoxin: _____
   _____

8. salmonella: _____
   _____

9. norovirus: _____
   _____

10. toxoplasmosis: _____
    _____

11. Department of Health: _____
    _____

12. food preparation guidelines: _____
    _____

Investigation 3.11A Dr. _____

Worksheet 3.11A P.____ Date:_____

Foodborne Pathogens Worksheet

Directions: Refer to your reading in Foodborne Pathogens to answer the following questions.

1. Foodborne Illness is commonly called _____.

2. To what U.S. government agency does the acronym "CDC" refer?
   _____

3. About how many foodborne diseases are recognized by the CDC?_____

4. What are the three major categories of foodborne illness?

   a. _____
   b. _____
   c. _____

5. What fraction of the total U.S. population gets food poisoning each year?
   _____

6. About how many people die from foodborne illnesses each year in the U.S.?
   _____

7. Name five bacterial foodborne illnesses.

   a. _____
   b. _____
   c. _____
   d. _____
   e. _____

8. What virus causes the most foodborne illness in the U.S.?
   _____

3.11A: Foodborne Pathogens Dr._____

page 2

9. How can anyone insure they do not contract hepatitis A?
_____

10. Why is it important for the physician to know which bacteria is causing the illness?
_____
_____

11. What is often the best test available to determine the pathogen causing the foodborne illness?
_____

12. What is the Mice Inoculation Test used for?
_____

13. What are the four basic rules of safe food preparation?
   a. _____
   b. _____
   c. _____
   d. _____

14. Name two ways that bacteria and parasites are similar.
   a. _____
   b. _____

15. Name three responsibilities physicians have in caring for their patients
   a. _____
   b. _____
   c. _____

Investigation 3.11B   Dr. _____

Food-borne Pathogen Case   P._____ Date_____

Vocabulary 1: Definitions

Directions: Use the text, a dictionary, or the internet to write a definition for each term.

1. abdominal cramps: _____
   _____

2. diarrhea: _____
   _____

3. vomiting: _____
   _____

4. fever: _____
   _____

5. joint pain: _____
   _____

6. food-borne pathogen: _____
   _____

7. antibiotic: _____
   _____

8. pathogenic parasite: _____
   _____

9. pathogenic virus: _____
   _____

10. pathogenic bacteria: _____
    _____

11. stool specimen: _____
    _____

12. dehydrated: _____
    _____

Investigation 3.11B   Dr. _____

Food-borne Pathogen Case   P. _____ Date _____

Vocabulary 2: Matching

Directions: Match the definitions on the right to the terms on the left.

1. _____ abdominal cramps
2. _____ diarrhea
3. _____ vomiting
4. _____ fever
5. _____ joint pain
6. _____ food-borne pathogen
7. _____ antibiotic
8. _____ pathogenic parasite
9. _____ pathogenic virus
10. _____ pathogenic bacteria
11. _____ stool specimen
12. _____ dehydrated

a. a virus having the capability of causing illness, such as norovirus & hepatitis A
b. an elevation of body temperature often signaling an infection; pyrexia
c. stomach pain
d. a poop sample; a tool for determining the cause of foodborne illness
e. pain limited to your shoulder, your knee, your elbow, and so on
f. condition where feces discharged in liquid form
g. condition with loss of 5% or more of your body fluid
h. emesis, regurgitation, or throwing up; stomach contents ejected through mouth or nose
i. any parasite with the potential to cause illness; examples are toxoplasma and trichinella
j. any bacteria, virus, fungi, or parasite capable of causing illness when ingested in food or water
k. medicine that inhibits the growth or kills bacteria
l. any bacteria capable of causing illness, such as staph aureus or salmonella

Investigation 3.11B

Food-borne Pathogen Case

Dr. _____

P. ____ Date: _____

Vocabulary 3: Sentences

Directions: Write a sentence using each term.

1. abdominal cramps: _____
   _____

2. diarrhea: _____
   _____

3. vomiting: _____
   _____

4. fever: _____
   _____

5. joint pain: _____
   _____

6. food-borne pathogen: _____
   _____

7. antibiotic: _____
   _____

8. pathogenic parasite: _____
   _____

9. pathogenic virus: _____
   _____

10. pathogenic bacteria: _____
    _____

11. stool specimen: _____
    _____

12. dehydrated: _____
    _____

Investigation 3.11B

Dr._____

3.11B: Foodborne Pathogens

P.____ Date:_____

Foodborne Pathogen Case

1. What are Grace's symptoms of her illness?

    a. _____

    b. _____

    c. _____

    d. _____

    e. _____

2. Which clues helped direct you to consider foodborne illness as the origin of Grace's sickness?

    a. _____

    b. _____

    c. _____

3. What was unusual about the timing of Grace's and her boyfriend's becoming sick?

    _____

4. Which two bacteria are candidates as the most likely pathogen in Grace's illness?

    a. _____

    b. _____

5. How are the two most likely bacterial pathogens treated differently?

    _____
    _____

6. Which test can you perform to identify the actual pathogen in this case?

    _____

Investigation 3.11B　　　　　　　　　　　　　　　　　　　　Dr._____

Worksheet 3.11B, page 2

7. The results of the stool sample test identify the pathogen as Salmonella. What should you do now?

   _____
   _____

8. Should you contact any public agency to report this food poisoning event?

   Circle your answer:　　　　　YES　　　　　NO

9. If yes, which agency should be contacted and why? If no, why not?

   _____
   _____
   _____

This case represents a dangerous habit many people display: leaving perishable foods without refrigeration for extended periods of time. Two good habits pertaining to pre-cooked chickens are:

1. Make sure the chicken is fully cooked; don't pick the lightest chicken in the batch. Also, look at the time stamp on the chicken; select one that has not been sitting out more than one hour.

2. When you get the chicken home, place it in the refrigerator immediately if you are not able to eat it right away.

Follow-up: As Grace's physician, you would call Grace to give her the results of the laboratory test. In this case you would also advise her that antibiotics are not recommended for this particular bacteria. You would then advise her that Salmonella illness usually lasts 5 to 7 days, and ask her to contact you if she does not feel better in a few more days because Salmonella in some people can revolve into a more serious condition.

Investigation 3.11AB

Crossword 3.11B **Foodborne Illness**

Dr._____   P.____ Date:_____

Directions: Use the highlighted terms in the chapter to solve the puzzle. Most clues come from the chapter text, some require outside investigation. Omit spaces or dashes between words.

Medical Investigation 101 - Hill & Griffith

ACROSS

4 the leading cause of foodborne death in the U.S.
5 instrument used to see very small organisms, such as bacteria
7 the result of taking a good history and physical exam, using appropriate tests, and considering all of the possibilities
9 measures taken to assure you do not catch a contagious disease or unnecessary injury
13 subjective or objective clues about a disease affecting a patient
15 sickness resulting from eating contaminated food
21 the definitive test for diagnosing botulism
22 breathed or eaten; taken into the body
24 to introduce a disease or a vaccine into a person
28 common foodborne bacteria having an incubatiion period of 6-72 hours and a usual duration of illness of 5-7 days
30 feces or poop
31 bacterial foodborne pathogen mostly commonly ingested from raw milk, poultry, and contaminated water
32 an organism that lives in or on a host and benefits at the expense of the host

DOWN

1 the term used for growing bacteria in a laboratory
2 medical term for patient having a weak natural system of protection of sickness
3 living microscopic organisms capable of growing without a host
6 organisms visible with electron microscope; incapable of surviving without a host
8 organisms that cause illness or disease
10 medical name for vomit
11 the time from when a pathogen is ingested until the patient shows symptoms
12 the agency to whom physicians report incidents of food poisoning
14 a medicine designed to control or kill illness-causing bacteria
16 foodborne illness caused by contaminated eggs, meat, poultry, and raw fruits and vegetables
17 the health of the entire population of the residents of the United States
18 come from animal muscles
19 an antibody that neutralizes the toxin of a causative agent
20 medical term for contamination by poop
23 the state occurring from excess sweating, vomiting, or diarrhea
25 rare, but very serious, food poisoning caused by improperly canned foods; caused by Clostridium botulinum
26 the foodborne pathogen causing more gastrointestinal illness than any other
27 things we do the same way over and over
29 acronym for Centers for Disease Control and Prevention

Investigation 3.12A

Dr. _____

Head Injury

P. _____ Date _____

Vocabulary 1: Definitions

Directions: Use the text, a dictionary, or the internet to write a definition for each term.

1. gravity: _____
   _____

2. inertia: _____
   _____

3. kinetic energy: _____
   _____

4. skull: _____
   _____

5. cerebral spinal fluid: _____
   _____

6. intracranial arterial bleed: _____
   _____

7. trephination: _____
   _____

8. neurosurgeon: _____
   _____

9. skull fracture: _____
   _____

10. concussion: _____
    _____

11. cerebral aneurysm: _____
    _____

Investigation 3.12A

Head Injury

Vocabulary 2: Matching

Dr. _____

P._____ Date_____

Directions: Match the definitions on the right to the medical terms on the left.

1. _____ gravity
2. _____ inertia
3. _____ kinetic energy
4. _____ skull
5. _____ cerebral spinal fluid
6. _____ intracranial arterial bleed
7. _____ trephination
8. _____ neurosurgeon
9. _____ skull fracture
10. _____ concussion
11. _____ cerebral aneurysm

a. a surgeon specializing in the brain, spinal cord, and nervous system
b. the force keeping us from floating into space
c. the boney covering of your brain
d. a crack in the boney covering of your brain
e. a serious medical emergency where bleeding causes pressure on the delicate brain tissue
f. a bulge or ballooning of a blood vessel in the brain that can leak or rupture
g. a traumatic brain injury usually caused by a blow to the head; common injury in contact sports
h. the energy possessed by an object due to its motion
i. surgical intervention for intracranial bleeding where a hole in cut or drilled in the skull to remove blood and release pressure on the brain
j. the tendency of an object to remain at rest or in motion unless acted upon by a force
k. clear, colorless body fluid found in the brain and spine; provides cushion and immunological protection to brain

Investigation 3.12A

Head Injury

Vocabulary 3: Sentences

Dr. _____

P. _____ Date _____

Directions: Use each term in a sentence.

1. gravity: _____
   _____

2. inertia: _____
   _____

3. kinetic energy: _____
   _____

4. skull: _____
   _____

5. cerebral spinal fluid: _____
   _____

6. intracranial arterial bleed: _____
   _____

7. trephination: _____
   _____

8. neurosurgeon: _____
   _____

9. skull fracture: _____
   _____

10. concussion: _____
    _____

11. cerebral aneurysm: _____
    _____

Investigation 3.12A Head Injury Dr._____

Worksheet 3.12A P.____Date_____

Head Injury

1. As you approached Alice and the other players untangled themselves and moved away, what three positive signs did you observe in Alice's condition?

    a. _____

    b. _____

    c. _____

2. As you quickly visually examined Alice as she lay on the floor, what things did you observe that concerned you?

    a. _____

    b. _____

    c. _____

3. Why didn't you take a complete history on this patient?
   _____

4. What were Alice's vital signs when taken by Liz and Graham?

    BP = _____ Pulse = _____ Respirations = _____/min

5. What is the normal range for resting blood pressure? _____/_____ mm/Hg

6. What is the normal pulse range for an athlete like Alice? _____ to _____ beats/min

7. What might explain Alice's blood pressure at the time it was taken following her injury?

   _____

Investigation 3.12A Head Injury Dr._____

Worksheet 3.12A, Page 2

8. **Do you think** the change in Alice's blood pressure could have triggered the bleeding in her brain? Why or Why Not?
    YES   NO   Why: _____
    _____
    _____

9. What is an aneurysm?
    _____
    _____

10. What is a cerebral aneurysm?
    _____
    _____
    _____

11. Do you think there could be any significance to the shaking of Alice's body that was observed while the bodies were still entangled on the floor? If so, what?
    _____
    _____

12. Why did you think it was necessary to quickly transport Alice to the hospital and have a neurosurgeon ready to examine her on arrival?
    _____
    _____
    _____
    _____

Investigation 3.12A Head Injury

Worksheet 3.12A – page 3

Dr._____

P.____ Date_____

13. What simple test can be performed to indicate whether or not a patient has probably sustained a bleeding event inside their skull that is putting pressure on the brain? How is the test performed?

_____
_____
_____

14. If the Pupil Reaction Test is positive in both eyes, meaning both pupils are fixed in dilation and not reactive to light, what does that most likely indicate in this patient?

_____

15. What is the name of the area, or lobe, of the brain that controls vision?

_____

16. Does it always mean there is potential brain damage if both eyes are fixed in a dilated state? Think about the last time you had a complete eye examination; did they do anything to your eyes?

_____
_____
_____
_____

17. Which two physician specialists from the list probably encounter the stress of treating emergencies most often?

    1. _____ 2. _____

18. You have had time to think about the level of stress you would enjoy dealing with in your medical career. Which specialty or specialties appeal most at this time to your sense of your desire and ability to deal with stress?

    1. _____ 2. _____

Investigation 3.12A Head Injury
Worksheet 3.12A – page 4   Dr._____

19. Looking back at your previous thoughts about how often various doctors encounter emergency situations, circle the frequency you think each of the following medical specialists encounter emergencies, where clear thinking and swift action is required.

   Rare   Occasional   Common   CARDIOLOGIST

   Rare   Occasional   Common   DERMATOLOGIST

   Rare   Occasional   Common   EMERGENCY ROOM PHYSICIAN

   Rare   Occasional   Common   OBSTETRICIAN

   Rare   Occasional   Common   PATHOLOGIST

   Rare   Occasional   Common   PODIATRIST

   Rare   Occasional   Common   ANESTHESIOLOGIST

   Rare   Occasional   Common   ORTHOPEDIST

   Rare   Occasional   Common   OPTHAMOLOGIST

   Rare   Occasional   Common   TRAUMA SURGEON

3.12 - Activity 1: Checking Pupil Reactivity

Required Supplies: Penlight or Flashlight (not a laser)

Directions: Follow the steps in order:

1. Lower the light level in the room if possible
2. Get a partner to test
3. Observe the pupil size of your test subject; both pupils should be approximately equal in size
4. Quickly shine the penlight or flashlight briefly (1 or 2 seconds) into their eye and observe the pupil constrict (get smaller)
5. Then shine the light away from the eye and watch the pupil get larger.
6. Repeat steps four (4) and five (5) on the other eye
7. What happened when you shined the light in your partner's eye?

_____

Investigation 3.12A Head Injury

Post-Script

Alice made it to the hospital emergency room and the neurosurgeon was waiting and ready to take over. He performed neurological tests and determined that Alice was, indeed, in danger of permanent brain damage if he did not relieve the pressure on her brain. He ordered that she be delivered immediately to the special procedures room so that he can perform emergency brain surgery.

Thanks to your medical curiosity about Alice's condition and your medical knowledge to know first, to look at her eyes, and second, to know the significance of her eyes appearing fixed and dilated, Alice came through her surgery well and suffered no permanent disabilities.

Do you think you might want to be a brain surgeon? Later in this chapter you will come across some activities you can use to find out.

Investigation 3.12A   Dr._____

Crossword 3.12A   **Head Injury**   P.____Date:_____

Directions: Use the highlighted terms in the chapter to solve the puzzle. Most clues come from the chapter text, some require outside investigation. Omit spaces or dashes between words.

ACROSS

1. bleeding from the brain inside the skull
4. weakness and ballooning within artery or vein; examples are brain and aorta
5. a temporary traumatic brain injury caused by jarring force; common injury in violent sports, such as football
7. the clear, colorless body fluid found in the brain and spine; cushions the brain within the skull
8. blood vessels returning de-oxygenated blood to the lungs
9. the colored part of your eye
11. the force that keeps our bodies from floating off into space
13. the boney protective cover of the brain
14. guides for successfully performing tasks the same way each time
17. members of the medical support team trained in managing victims of trauma
21. according to Newton's First Law, the property that matter remains at rest or in motion unless acted upon by an external forrce
22. the control center of the human body; sits inside the skull
23. the father of Neurosurgery
25. a sequence of actions regularly followed: the way you choose to accomplish a frequently performed task
27. a physician who diagnoses and treats brain and other central nervous system problems
28. the area inside the iris where light enters the eye

DOWN

2. the red liquid that circulates in arteries and veins, carrying oxygen to and carbon dioxide from the tissues
3. weakness and ballooning of a blood vessel in the brain; can rupture spontaneously to produce an intracranial bleed
6. the absence of bacteria and other germs
10. the force of blood pushing against our arteries at contraction and relaxation of our heart
12. a surgical procedure where a hole is drilled through the skull to release blood following a brain injury
15. a scientist who studies the function of the nervous system
16. a crack or break in a bone
18. the active exchange of oxygen and carbon dioxide between the atmosphere and our bodies
19. an injury occurring from a blow, cut, or penetrating wound
20. energy possessed by virtue of being in motion
24. the capacity to endure pain or hardship; the increased need for a higher dose of a medicine over time
26. the rate at which your heart beats

Investigation 3.12B

Dr. _____

The Eye

P._____ Date_____

Vocabulary 1A: Definitions

Directions: Use the text, a dictionary, or the internet to write a definition for each term.

1. cornea: _____
   _____

2. transparent: _____
   _____

3. astigmatism: _____
   _____

4. Lasik: _____
   _____

5. myopia: _____
   _____

6. hyperopia: _____
   _____

7. corneal abrasion: _____
   _____

8. iris: _____
   _____

9. pupil: _____
   _____

10. lens: _____
    _____

11. cataract: _____
    _____

12. bifocals: _____
    _____

223

Investigation 3.12B					Dr. _____

The Eye					P. _____ Date _____

Vocabulary 2A: Matching

Directions: Match the definitions on the right to the medical terms on the left.

1. _____ cornea
2. _____ transparent
3. _____ astigmatism
4. _____ Lasik
5. _____ myopia
6. _____ hyperopia
7. _____ corneal abrasion
8. _____ iris
9. _____ pupil
10. _____ lens
11. _____ cataract
12. _____ bifocals

a. laser vision correction for myopia, hyperopia, and astigmatism
b. eyeglasses or contact lens having two areas, one for near and one for far vision
c. the black area inside the iris that regulates the amount of light entering the eye
d. an eye defect where light focuses behind the retina; farsightedness
e. allowing light to pass through such that objects behind can be seen
f. it focuses the light rays passing through it onto the retina and changes the focal distance by changing shape
g. the round area behind the cornea that adjusts the opening of the pupil and gives eyes their color
h. a condition where the eye's lens becomes progressively opaque, resulting in blurred vision
i. the transparent layer forming the front of the eye
j. a scratch on the cornea of the eye
k. visual defect where light is focused in front of the retina; nearsightedness
l. a misshaped eyeball that isn't round enough, but instead too egg-shaped to properly focus light evenly

Investigation 3.12B

The Eye

Vocabulary 3A: Sentences

Directions: Use each term in a sentence.

1. cornea: _____
   _____

2. transparent: _____
   _____

3. astigmatism: _____
   _____

4. Lasik: _____
   _____

5. myopia: _____
   _____

6. hyperopia: _____
   _____

7. corneal abrasion: _____
   _____

8. iris: _____
   _____

9. pupil: _____
   _____

10. lens: _____
    _____

11. cataract: _____
    _____

12. bifocals: _____
    _____

Dr. _____

P. _____ Date _____

Investigation 3.12B   Dr. _____

The Eye   P._____ Date_____

Vocabulary 1B: Definitions

Directions: Use the text, a dictionary, or the internet to write a definition for each term.

1. progressive: _____
   _____

2. retina: _____
   _____

3. rods: _____
   _____

4. cones: _____
   _____

5. detached retina: _____
   _____

6. ophthalmoscope: _____
   _____

7. macula: _____
   _____

8. macular degeneration: _____
   _____

9. optic nerve : _____
   _____

10. glaucoma: _____
    _____

11. thalamus: _____
    _____

12. occipital lobe: _____
    _____

Investigation 3.12B

The Eye

Vocabulary 2B: Matching

Dr. _____

P._____ Date_____

Directions: Match the definitions on the right to the medical terms on the left.

1. _____ progressive
2. _____ retina
3. _____ rods
4. _____ cones
5. _____ detached retina
6. _____ ophthalmoscope
7. _____ macula
8. _____ macular degeneration
9. _____ optic nerve
10. _____ glaucoma
11. _____ thalamus
12. _____ occipital lobe

a. the layer at the back of the eye where the visual image forms
b. an instrument for examining the retina and other parts of the eye
c. condition where retina becomes separated from underlying tissue, causing loss of vision in affected area
d. brain matter that acts as relay of left and right eye visual input
e. second pair of cranial nerves, transmits impulses from retina to brain
f. the brain lobe responsible for processing visual input
g. photoreceptors in the retina responsible for color vision
h. a condition of increased pressure within the eyeball that causes gradual loss of vision
i. happening or developing gradually, or proceeding step by step
j. the area of the retina most packed with cones and having the keenest vision
k. the photoreceptors in the retina responsible for vision at low light levels in only black and white
l. an age-related degenerative eye condition affecting the central part of the retina resulting in distortion or loss of vision

Investigation 3.12B

The Eye

Dr. _____

P____ Date:_____

Vocabulary 3B: Sentences

Directions: Use each term in a sentence.

1. progressive: _____
   _____

2. retina: _____
   _____

3. rods: _____
   _____

4. cones: _____
   _____

5. detached retina: _____
   _____

6. ophthalmoscope: _____
   _____

7. macula: _____
   _____

8. macular degeneration: _____
   _____

9. optic nerve : _____
   _____

10. glaucoma: _____
    _____

11. thalamus: _____
    _____

12. occipital lobe: _____
    _____

Investigation 3.12B The Eye　　　　　　　　　　　　　Dr._____

Worksheet 3.12B1　　　　　　　　　　　　　　　　　P.___Date:_____

The Eye

Directions: Answer the following questions about the eye.

1. What is the pupil? _____

2. What is the iris? _____

3. What is the function of the iris?_____

4. What is the eye lens? _____

5. What is the function of your lens? _____

6. How does the lens focus both close and far away objects? _____

7. Why do people over age 40 often wear reading glasses or bifocal glasses for near and far sight? _____

8. What eye structure protects the lens from being easily scratched when we rub our eyes? What else does it do? _____

Investigation 3.12 B   Dr._____

Worksheet 3.12B1, page 2

9. What is the cornea? _____
   _____

10. What common injury occurs to the cornea? _____

11. What is the retina? _____
    _____

12. Name two types of specialized cells located on the retina? Describe their functions.
    _____
    _____

13. In what orientation do images appear on our retinas? _____
    _____

14. Where do the upside-down images seem to get turned right side up?
    _____

15. Name two common injuries that occur to the retina, mostly in people past age 50?
    a. _____
    b. _____

16. How does an image move from the retina to your brain? _____
    _____

17. How might an injury to the back of the head cause impaired vision or a ruptured aneurysm result in fixed and dilated pupils? _____
    _____
    _____

Investigation 3.12B   Dr._____

Crossword 3.12B   **The Eye**   P.____Date:_____

Directions: Use the highlighted terms in the chapter to solve the puzzle. Most clues come from the chapter text, some require outside investigation. Omit spaces or dashes between words.

Medical Investigation 101 - Hill & Griffith

ACROSS

3 photoreceptor cells responsible for color vision; work best in bright light conditions
6 eye surgery to cornea correcting myopia, hyperopia, and astigmatism
7 the first point of light beam eye contact
8 the white outer layer of the eyeball; continuous with the cornea at the front of the eye
10 disease of the optic nerve caused by excessively high pressure of the fluid inside the eye
13 a progressive clouding of the lens; eye gradually loses its ability to focus light toward the retina; correctible with surgery
14 photoreceptor cells concentrated at the peripheral edges of the retina; work best in low light conditions
15 far-sightedness; the light beam is not yet in focus when it reaches the retina
18 near-sightedness; the light beam focus point before reaching the retina
19 sends electrical impulses from optic disc to the thalamus and then occipital lobe of the brain
21 our organs of vision
22 the portion of the retina where the optic nerve attaches at the optic disc
24 the movie screen of the eye; the image is upside down
25 lens of glasses that have two corrections; one for near visiion and one for distance vision
26 the portion of the retina having the greatest acuity

DOWN

1 the least common eye color; requires double recessive gene traits
2 the area of the brain that processes image signals from the optic nerves andflips the retinal image to right-side-up
3 a scratch on the eye cornea
4 progressive degeneration of the macula within the retina
5 the entire area the eyes can see without moving the eyes
9 medical eye emergency; can result in permanent loss of vision
11 clearness of vision
12 the membrane overing the front of the eye and lines the inside of the eyelids; pink eye irritates this
16 an imperfection in the shape of the eye affecting how the eye focuses light; correctable with glasses or surgery
17 the pigmented, or colored part of the eye
20 the open space in the middle of the iris through which light passes on its way to the retina
23 hopefully bends light in the eye such that it focuses at a single point on the retina

Investigation 3.13A   Dr. _____

The Brain   P._____ Date_____

Vocabulary 1A: Definitions

Directions: Use the text, a dictionary, or the internet to write a definition for each term.

1. neuroanatomist: _____
   _____

2. gross: _____
   _____

3. hemisphere: _____
   _____

4. lobes: _____
   _____

5. neural plasticity: _____
   _____

6. neurons: _____
   _____

7. neurologist: _____
   _____

8. stroke: _____
   _____

9. frontal lobe: _____
   _____

10. parietal lobes: _____
    _____

11. cortical homunculus: _____
    _____

12. sensation: _____
    _____

Investigation 3.13A

The Brain

Vocabulary 2A: Matching

Dr. _____

P._____ Date_____

Directions: Match the definitions on the right to the terms on the left.

1. _____ neuroanatomist
2. _____ gross
3. _____ hemisphere
4. _____ lobes
5. _____ neural plasticity
6. _____ neurons
7. _____ neurologist
8. _____ stroke
9. _____ frontal lobe
10. _____ parietal lobes
11. _____ cortical homunculus
12. _____ sensation

a. the sensory and motor neurological maps of the anatomical divisions of the body located in the brain
b. a physician who specializes in treating diseases of the nervous system
c. the left or right half of the brain, connected by the corpus callosum
d. the area of the brain lying directly behind the forehead
e. the scientist who studies the anatomy and organization of the nervous system
f. specialized cells that transmit nerve impulses in the brain and throughout the body
g. lobes positioned above the occipital lobes serving as the highest level of sensory and motor awareness
h. the divisions of the cerebrum of our brain in four distinct functional areas
i. a feeling or perception of motion or sensation of contact with the body
j. the brain's neurons ability to learn and adapt to an individual's needs regardless of their place within the brain
k. the sudden death of brain cells caused by blockage of blood flow or rupture of an artery in the brain
l. large enough to be visualized with only the naked eye

Investigation 3.13A Dr. _____

The Brain P._____Date_____

Vocabulary 3A: Sentences

Directions: Use each term in a sentence.

1. neuroanatomist: _____
   _____

2. gross: _____
   _____

3. hemisphere: _____
   _____

4. lobes: _____
   _____

5. neural plasticity: _____
   _____

6. neurons: _____
   _____

7. neurologist: _____
   _____

8. stroke: _____
   _____

9. frontal lobe: _____
   _____

10. parietal lobes: _____
    _____

11. cortical homunculus: _____
    _____

12. sensation: _____
    _____

Investigation 3.13A Dr. _____

The Brain P._____ Date_____

Vocabulary 1B: Definitions

Directions: Use the text, a dictionary, or the internet to write a definition for each term.

1. motor: _____
   _____

2. temporal lobe: _____
   _____

3. occipital lobe: _____
   _____

4. cerebellum: _____
   _____

5. coordination: _____
   _____

6. brain stem: _____
   _____

7. action potential: _____
   _____

8. axons: _____
   _____

9. dendrites: _____
   _____

10. inhibition: _____
    _____

11. backpropogation: _____
    _____

12. artificial intelligence: _____
    _____

Investigation 3.13A

The Brain

Vocabulary 2B: Matching

Directions: Match the definitions on the right to the terms on the left.

1. _____ motor
2. _____ temporal lobe
3. _____ occipital lobe
4. _____ cerebellum
5. _____ coordination
6. _____ brain stem
7. _____ action potential
8. _____ axons
9. _____ dendrites
10. _____ inhibition
11. _____ backpropagation
12. _____ artificial intelligence

a. nerve impulses that stimulate a change in another neuron or cause a muscle cell to contract
b. the area of the brain located above your ears receiving sensory information about sounds and understanding speech
c. a feeling of restraint or blockage; blocking an impulse or limiting an action
d. having to do with motion or action; example: stimulating a muscle to contract
e. the ability to use various parts of the body together smoothly and efficiently
f. the use of computer systems to perform tasks normally requiring human intelligence
g. the area of the brain responsible for coordination of muscular activity
h. the long threadlike portion of a neuron that conducts impulses from the cell body to other neurons
i. the visual processing center of our brain
j. adjusting a system by comparing to desired output and adjusting until difference is minimized
k. the part of the brain controlling and regulating vital body functions including respiration, heart rate, and blood pressure
l. short neuron extensions that receive impulses from axons at synapses and transmit to the cell body

Investigation 3.13A

The Brain

Vocabulary 3B: Sentences

Dr. _____

P._____ Date_____

Directions: Use each term in a sentence.

1. motor: _____
_____

2. temporal lobe: _____
_____

3. occipital lobe: _____
_____

4. cerebellum: _____
_____

5. coordination: _____
_____

6. brain stem: _____
_____

7. action potential: _____
_____

8. axons: _____
_____

9. dendrites: _____
_____

10. inhibition: _____
_____

11. backpropogation: _____
_____

12. artificial intelligence: _____
_____

Investigation 3.13A: Dr._____

Worksheet 3.13A1 P.____ Date:_____

The Brain

Directions: Answer the following questions based on your reading of chapter 3.13A.

1. What does an 'anatomist' study?
   _____

2. What does a 'neuroanatomist' study?
   _____

3. What name describes the two sides of your brain?
   _____

4. Each brain hemisphere contains how many lobes?
   _____

5. Name the lobes of your cerebral cortex:

   a. _____

   b. _____

   c. _____

   d. _____

6. What name do we give the ability of the brain regain normal function following major brain injury? _____

7. What signs should you recognize and attribute to a possible stroke?
   _____
   _____

8. Which lobe of the brain controls your emotions, passions, and hopes?
   _____

9. What is the primary function of the Occipital Lobe?
   _____

10. Why does each parietal lobe contain <u>two</u> invisible diagrams of your entire body?
    _____

Investigation 3.13A The Brain　　　　　　　　　　　　　　Dr._____

Worksheet 3.13A1, page 2

11. About what percent of the information collected by the retina is forwarded by optic nerve to the brain? _____ %

12. Which brain area, not a lobe, bears responsibility for coordination of all muscle movement in your body? _____

13. List at least three functions of the brain stem.

    a. _____
    b. _____
    c. _____
    d. _____

14. How many cells does your brain contain? _____

15. What is an "action potential"?
    _____

16. Groups of neurons, along with their axons and dendrites, make up nerve systems known as _____ _____.

17. Briefly describe the concept of "backpropogation".
    _____
    _____

18. Describe "artificial intelligence" (you can look it up on the internet)
    _____
    _____

19. The symptoms of a stroke depend upon what area of the brain stops receiving blood flow and oxygen. Where would you look for a stroke that paralyzes the left arm?
    _____

20. Can you think of an evolutionary advantage for the cross wiring of the brain so the right hemisphere has primary control of the left side of the body?
    _____
    _____

Investigation 3.13A The Brain   Dr._____

Worksheet 3.13A2   P.____Date_____

Basic Brain Anatomy

Directions: Label the parts of the brain. Try to do it without looking at the previous diagram. Compare your answers with the diagram and make any necessary corrections.

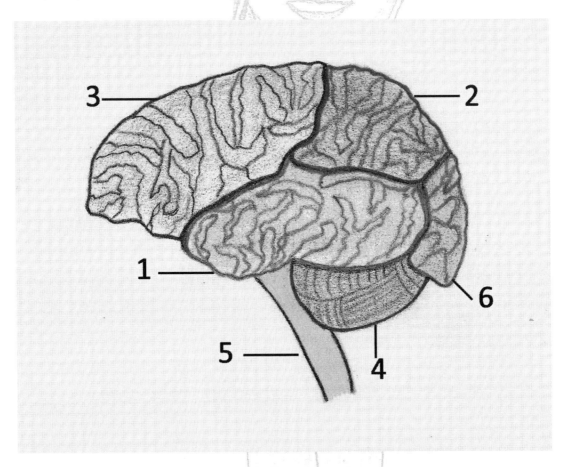

Directions: Write the name of the brain part corresponding to each number.

1. _____
2. _____
3. _____
4. _____
5. _____
6. _____

Investigation 3.13A   Dr._____

Brain Worksheet 2   P.____Date:_____

Right vs Left Brain Activity

Directions: Place an R in the space to identify Right Brain Activity. Place an L in the space to indicate a Left Brain Activity. Refer back to the diagram if needed.

_____ Science & Math   _____ Intuition

_____ Music Awareness   _____ Language

_____ Numbers Skills   _____ Logic

_____ Imagination   _____ Analytic thought

_____ 3-D Forms Visualization   _____ Holistic thought

_____ Right-hand control   _____ Reasoning

_____ Left-hand control   _____ Art Awareness

Investigation 3.13A   Dr._____

Crossword 3.13A1   **The Brain**   P.____ Date:_____

Directions: Use the highlighted terms in the chapter to solve the puzzle. Most clues come from the chapter text, some require outside investigation. Omit spaces or dashes between words.

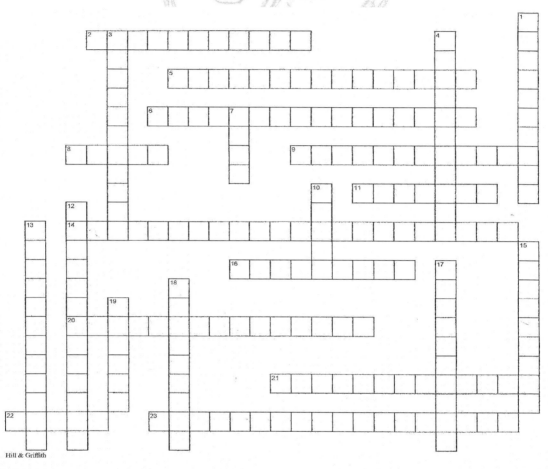

ACROSS

2 a feeling of restraint or blockage; blocking an impulse or limiting an action
5 adjusting a system by comparing to desired output and adjusting until the difference is minimized
6 the brain's neurons ability to learn and adapt to an individual's needs regardless of their place within the brain
8 large enough to be visualized with only the naked eye
9 the area of the brain located above your ears receiving sensory information about sounds and understanding speech
11 specialized cells that transmit nerve impulses in the brain and throughout the body
14 the use of computer systems to perform tasks normally requiring human intelligence
16 short neuron extensions the receive impulses from axons at synapses and transmit to the cell body
20 nerve impulses that stimulate a change in another neuron or cause a muscle cell to contract
21 the visual processing center of our brain
22 the divisions of the cerebrum of our brain into four distinct functional areas
23 the sensory and motor neurological maps of the anatomical divisions of the body located in the brain

DOWN

1 the left or right half of the brain, connected by the corpus callosum
3 a physician who specializes in treating diseases of the neurological system
4 the area of the brain lying directly behind the forehead
7 the long threadlike portion of a neuron that conducts impulses from the cell body to other neurons
10 having to do with motion or action; example, stimulating a muscle to contract
12 the brain lobes located above the occipital lobes serving as the highest level of sensory and motor awareness
13 the ability to use various parts of the body together smoothly and efficiently
15 the part of the brain controlling and regulating vital body functions including respiration, heart rate, and blood pressure
17 the area of the brain responsible for coordination of muscular activity
18 a feeling or perception of motion or sensation of contact with the body
19 the sudden death of brain cells caused by blockage of blood flow or rupture of an artery in the brain large enough to be visualized with only the naked eye

Investigation 3.13A

Crossword 3.13A2 The Brain

Directions: Use the highlighted terms in the chapter to solve the puzzle. Most clues come from the chapter text, some require outside investigation. Omit spaces or dashes between words.

Medical Investigation 101 - Hill & Griffith

ACROSS

1 doctors who operate on the brain
7 the arrangement of our neural networks at a particular time
8 send signals from their cell body towards the synapse
9 brain area processing visual input from your eyes
10 receive input from axons at synapses and send to their neural cell body
11 the portion of your brain controlling your emotions, determination, passions, and hopes
14 type of brain cells that direct signals where you want them to go
19 the "wires" in the brain that transport electrical signals throughout the body; they have the ability to learn and adapt to an individual's needs
20 used in scanners to observe increased activity in various parts of the brain
28 the scientist who studies human anatomy
30 doctors who study the brain and diagnose abnormalities
31 to change in order to improve performance
32 the four sections of the human cerebrum
33 located below cerebellum; manages your autonomic functions such as breathing, digestion, and heart rate
35 the relative important of a piece of data compared to another
36 to become different during the process of growth or development
37 the type of processes used to perform work inside the brain

DOWN

2 the scientist who studies the human brain
3 the way neurons decide how to adjust their sensitivity to inputs
4 a blockage of an artery or the rupture of a blood vessel in the brain resulting in disability or death
5 a negative input or effect
6 how neurons work together
12 the ability of computers to perform tasks normally requiring human intelligence
13 the brain's appearance from looking at the outside
15 the ability of childrens brains to heal following injury
16 medical terminology meaning large enough to study using only your eyes
17 a pulse of electrical current that travels through the neurons of brain cells
18 a test where a fine needle removes a sample of abnormal tissue to determine the presence or absence of cancer cells
21 brain area maintaining highest level of sensory and motor awareness of all your body's sensations and movement
22 the number of neural connections in a given space that may define one's ability to perform a task
23 to rearrange the settings or elements; the constant adjustment of our neural networks
24 area that manages the coordination of all muscular activity of your body
25 the tangled-rope appearing brain surface of the parietal, temporal, and occipital lobes
26 one half or one side of the brain
27 brain area that manages your hearing and speech
29 the view visualized looking from the side
34 the period of our development when our cells differentiate, multiply, and interconnect

Investigation 3.13B

Dr. _____

Normal or Abnormal?

P. _____ Date _____

Vocabulary 1: Definitions

Directions: Use the text, a dictionary, or the internet to write a definition for each term.

1. thermostat: _____
   _____

2. closed loop system: _____
   _____

3. open loop system: _____
   _____

4. extract: _____
   _____

5. calories: _____
   _____

6. adaptive controllers: _____
   _____

7. pacemaker: _____
   _____

8. conferences: _____
   _____

9. REM sleep: _____
   _____

10. Non-REM sleep: _____
    _____

11. Biological clock: _____
    _____

12. metformin: _____
    _____

Investigation 3.13B

Normal or Abnormal?

Vocabulary 2: Matching

Dr. _____

P. _____ Date _____

Directions: Match the descriptions on the right to the terms on the left.

1. _____ thermostat
2. _____ closed loop system
3. _____ open loop system
4. _____ extract
5. _____ calories
6. _____ adaptive controllers
7. _____ pacemaker
8. _____ conferences
9. _____ REM sleep
10. _____ non-REM sleep
11. _____ biological clock
12. _____ metformin

a. meetings attended by physicians to update their knowledge as part of their commitment to lifelong learning
b. a control system having set inputs but no measure of the output
c. our innate mechanism that controls our individual timing and behaviors, and physiological states and processes
d. a control system that measures output, compares that measurement to the desired output, and uses the difference to dictate what happens next
e. an oral medicine used to improve blood sugar control in type II diabetics by helping the body utilize insulin more efficiently
f. a unit of heat used to indicate the amount of energy foods will produce in the human body
g. the dreamless phase of sleep where breathing and heart rate are slow and regular
h. electronic device implanted inside the body to control the heart rate
i. to remove or utilize
j. a controller that regulates or activates a device when temperature reaches a certain point
k. rapid eye movement sleep that occurs at intervals where dreaming occurs and pulse, breathing, and movement increase
l. advanced controllers capable of complex decision-making and capable of learning

245

Investigation 3.13B

Normal or Abnormal?

Vocabulary 3: Sentences

Dr. _____

P. _____ Date _____

Directions: Use each term in a complete sentence.

1. thermostat: _____
   _____

2. closed loop system: _____
   _____

3. open loop system: _____
   _____

4. extract: _____
   _____

5. calories: _____
   _____

6. adaptive controllers: _____
   _____

7. pacemaker: _____
   _____

8. conferences: _____
   _____

9. REM sleep: _____
   _____

10. Non-REM sleep: _____
    _____

11. Biological clock: _____
    _____

12. metformin: _____
    _____

Investigation 3.13B Dr._____

Worksheet 3.13B P:____ Date:_____

Reflections: Normal or Abnormal

Directions: Reflect on your reading of investigation 3.14A to answer the following questions.

1. Which area of the brain controls and regulates body temperature?
   _____

2. Which body system acts as our body's furnace?
   _____

3. When our body extracts calories from food, into what is that energy converted?
   _____

4. Which specialty of medicine focuses on the ways the human body regulates itself and on diseases that affect that control?
   _____

5. What electronic device is utilized to control the electrical impulses of the heart?
   _____

6. What does any 'normal value' in the human body require?
   _____

7. What are two purposes of sleep?
   a. _____
   b. _____

8. What are the two main categories of sleep?
   a. _____
   b. _____

9. During which phase of sleep do we dream?
   _____

Investigation 3.13B   Dr._____
Worksheet 3.13B, Page 2

10. What special sleep-related skill do dolphins, porpoises, and penguins have?
    _____
    _____

11. Why do reptiles probably NOT dream about humans?
    _____

12. The fact that we get tired and awake at pretty much the same time each day is related to the functioning of our _____ _____

13. Name four types of life events that can cause disruption of our sleep cycle.
    a. _____
    b. _____
    c. _____
    d. _____

14. What two conditions are necessary in order to maintain a healthy sleep schedule?
    a. _____
    b. _____

15. Do you sleep well and feel rested most mornings? If yes, why do you think that happens? If no, which of the necessary conditions would you like to improve?
    _____
    _____
    _____
    _____

16. About how many years longer is the life expectancy for women longer than for men in the United States? _____ years

17. Name two methods that may prove useful in extending lifespan.
    a. _____
    b. _____

18. Which country currently has the longest average lifespan? _____

Investigation 3.13B

Crossword 3.13B Normal or Abnormal

Dr._____ P.____Date:_____

Directions: Use the highlighted terms in the chapter to solve the puzzle. Most clues come from the chapter text, some require outside investigation. Omit spaces or dashes between words.

Medical Investigation 101 - Hill & Griffith

ACROSS

2 type of animal incapable of REM sleep
6 a piece of genetic material that can be altered, or modified, to change the genetic code of a species
7 the phase of sleep where rapid eye movement occurs; the portion of sleep when we dream
11 an electronic device controlling the beating of the heart
13 a system that measures its output, compares measurement to a set desired point, then uses that difference to dictate what happens next
14 to influence or change controls, such as changing the lifespan of a human

DOWN

1 our natural control system which readies us to sleep each night
3 units of heat energy
4 the study of the way the body regulates its autonomic functions
5 a system having set inputs but no measure of the output and no ability to compensate for external factors
8 to remove or pull out, such as our bodies removing energy from our food
9 a medicine used in the treatment of diabetes that appears to have the potential of slowing down the aging process in humans
10 device sensing temperature change and sending signal to furnace to send heat
12 the last name of the doctor who in 1993 discovered how to double the lifespan and quality of life of a worm

Investigation 3.14A/B

The Final Case/Circle of Life

Vocabulary 1: Definitions

Dr. _____

P._____Date_____

Directions: Use the text, a dictionary, or the internet to write a definition for each term.

1. trends: _____
   _____

2. metastatic: _____
   _____

3. chemotherapy: _____
   _____

4. radiation therapy: _____
   _____

5. immune system: _____
   _____

6. Dr. Jennifer Doudna: _____
   _____

7. CRISPR: _____
   _____

8. circle of life: _____
   _____

9. death: _____
   _____

10. medical directive: _____
    _____

11. euthanasia: _____
    _____

Investigation 3.14A/B

The Final Case/Circle of Life

Vocabulary 2: Matching

Dr. _____

P._____ Date_____

Directions: Match the descriptions on the right to the terms on the left.

1. _____ trends
2. _____ metastatic
3. _____ chemotherapy
4. _____ radiation therapy
5. _____ immune system
6. _____ Dr. Jennifer Doudna
7. _____ CRISPR
8. _____ circle of life
9. _____ death
10. _____ medical directive
11. _____ euthanasia

a. the end of life
b. a genome editing tool that modifies DNA to correct undesirable traits or mutations
c. the treatment of disease, especially cancer, using x-rays and other forms of radiation
d. to spread out, as cancer often spreads from primary site to other organs
e. a document, also called a living will, that specifies what actions should be taken regarding one's health when they are no longer capable of making those decisions
f. a general change in a situation or way people are behaving
g. the symbolic representation of birth, survival, and death, followed by new life
h. treatment of illness, especially cancer, by use of cytotoxic chemicals and other drugs
i. our body's defense against organisms and other invaders
j. the painless killing of a patient suffering from an incurable and painful disease
k. a professor at UC Berkeley and a primary investigator of CRISPR

Investigation 3.14A/B

The Final Case/Circle of Life

Vocabulary 3: Sentences

Dr. _____

P. _____ Date _____

Directions: Use each term in a complete sentence.

1. trends: _____
   _____

2. metastatic: _____
   _____

3. chemotherapy: _____
   _____

4. radiation therapy: _____
   _____

5. immune system: _____
   _____

6. Dr. Jennifer Doudna: _____
   _____

7. CRISPR: _____
   _____

8. circle of life: _____
   _____

9. death: _____
   _____

10. medical directive: _____
    _____

11. euthanasia: _____
    _____

Investigation 3.14A: Final Case　　　　　　　　　　Dr. _____

Worksheet 3.14A　　　　　　　　　　　　　　　　　P.____Date_____

Reflections

Directions: Reflect on your reading of this investigation to answer the following questions.

1. In what way are cancer cells different from normal cells?
   _____
   _____

2. Name three possible treatments for cancer:
   a. _____
   b. _____
   c. _____

3. What is the negative aspect of treating cancer with chemotherapy drugs and radiation?
   _____

4. DNA is an acronym for:_____

5. Where can DNA be found? _____

6. What is the name of the leading scientist in CRISPRS technology?
   _____

7. What does the acronym CRISPR stand for?
   _____

8. Name three causes of DNA mistakes or defects:
   a. _____
   b. _____
   c. _____

Reflections, Investigation 3.14A   Dr._____

Side 2

9. Briefly summarize how CRISPRS works?

_____
_____
_____
_____

10. Explain how the advance in technology has both helped and harmed life on Earth.

_____
_____
_____

11. How do you feel about our potential ability to modify the DNA of children stricken with genetic disorders? Do you feel we should be changing the natural order? Why or why not?

_____
_____
_____
_____
_____

12. Write a paragraph addressing your feelings about the moral obligation of scientists concerning potential misuses of CRISTRS technology in the future.

_____
_____
_____
_____
_____
_____

Investigation 3.14B: Final Case

Worksheet 3.14B

Dr._____

P.____Date_____

Reflections

Directions: Answer the following based on your reading of Investigation 3.14B: Final Case.

1. Why is the "Circle of Life" inevitable for every living thing?

   _____

   _____

   _____

2. What does it mean for a patient to be 'terminal'?

   _____

   _____

   _____

3. What is one of the most difficult duties physicians have?

   _____

   _____

   _____

4. Do all patients and their families agree on end of life decisions? Explain

   _____

   _____

   _____

5. What is a 'medical directive'?

   _____

   _____

6. Since we never know which day will be our last day living on this Earth, what can we do to enhance our lives and those of our friends and family?

   _____

   _____

   _____

   _____

Investigation 3.14A/B   Dr._____

Crossword 3.14A/B   Final Case / Circle of Life   P.____ Date_____

Directions: Use the highlighted terms in the chapter to solve the puzzle. Most clues come from the chapter text, some require outside investigation. Omit spaces or dashes between words.

Medical Investigation 101 - Hill & Griffith

ACROSS

2 cancer that spreads throughout the body
4 cancer that came back
5 something new made by combining or modifying parts into a new whole
8 the treatment of cancer using radioactive materials
12 its acronym is DNA
13 the popular courses of action at a given time
15 the acronym for Clusters of Regularly Interspaced Short Palindromic Repeats; used recently in Brazil to modify malaria-carrying mosquitos
16 all of the possible candidates from a group; all diseases or all possible treatments

DOWN

1 tools for determining the degree of medical care desired by a patient at or near the end of their life
3 the painless assisted death of a patient suffering an incurable terminal illness; not legal in most U.S. states
6 the study of and treatment of cancer
7 the treatment of cancer with 'poisons'
9 the last name of the scientist who led the development of CRISPERS
10 our body's ability to identify and kill enemy cells without damaging our normal cells
11 chains of these make proteins
14 the set of chromosomes in each of our cells

Investigation 3.15   Dr. _____

Looking Deeper   P._____ Date_____

Vocabulary 1: Definitions

Directions: Use the text, a dictionary, or the internet to write a definition for each term.

1. history & physical: _____

2. differential diagnosis: _____

3. experience: _____

4. art of medical practice: _____

5. science of medical practice: _____

6. 5-whys: _____

7. Write an example of deeper thinking using the "5-Whys":

    a. _____

    b. _____

    c. _____

    d. _____

    e. _____

Investigation 3.15

Looking Deeper

Vocabulary 2: Matching

Dr. _____

P._____Date_____

Directions: Match the descriptions on the right to the terms on the left.

1. _____ history & physical
2. _____ differential diagnosis
3. _____ experience
4. _____ art of medical practice
5. _____ science of medical practice
6. _____ 5-whys

a. familiarity with a skill or field of knowledge acquired over month or years, presumably resulting in additional expertise in that field
b. the part of medical practice based on actual scientific knowledge
a. the part of the patient visit where the physician learns about the changes in the patient's health and the observations that help make the diagnosis
c. the part of medical practice based on experience and intuition
d. the list of possible causes of the symptoms and objective findings
e. a method to explore more fully the causes and effects of a particular problem

Investigation 3.15 Dr. _____

Looking Deeper P._____Date_____

Vocabulary 3: Sentences

Directions: Use each term in a complete sentence. Then write another example using 5-whys.

1. history & physical: _____

2. differential diagnosis:_____

3. experience: _____

4. art of medical practice: _____

5. science of medical practice: _____

6. 5-whys: _____

7. Write <u>another</u> example of deeper thinking using the "5-Whys":

    a. _____

    b. _____

    c. _____

    d. _____

    e. _____

Investigation 3.15   Dr._____

Crossword 3.15   Looking Deeper/ 5 Whys   P.____ Date:_____

Directions: Use the highlighted terms in the chapter to solve the puzzle. Most clues come from the chapter text, some require outside investigation. Omit spaces or dashes between words.

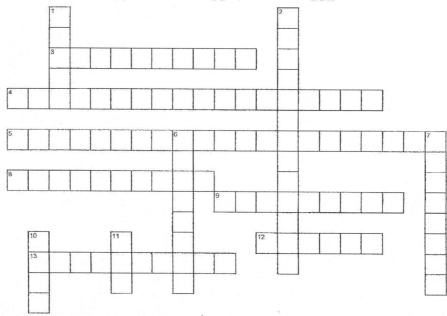

Medical Investigation 101 - Hill & Griffith

ACROSS

3 the maintenance and improvement of the physical and mental health of your patients
4 background informtion obtained from the patient AND information gained from your examination of the patient
5 a list of all known possible causes of the patient's problem
8 the side of your brain having the ability to think about, analyze, and synthesize all of the information about their patient's medical problem
9 the side of your brain where you use your knowledge of anatomy, physiology, and pathology to develop a differential diagnosis
12 last name of the "King of Japanese Inventors"
13 knowledge learned from seeing and performing procedures or having seen patients having similar problems

DOWN

1 the name of the trick for thinking deeper
2 a formal, systematic inquiry in the problem
6 the use of rational judgement or intelligence
7 subjective and objective clues that help the investigation of a patient's medical problem
10 an evaluation that gives objective information about a patient's medical condition
11 the expression of the creative process; original thoughts or feelings; how you apply your skills for the benefit of your patients

Post-Script

Congratulations! You have successfully completed a journey into the world of the medical practitioner. If you completed all of the assignments, you earned the Certificate of Completion of Medical Investigation 101 on the final page. You may carefully remove the certificate from the workbook, add your name, frame, and hang proudly on your wall. You now have a better understanding of the thought process required to solve the medical investigations so important and meaningful to your patients' well-being. This same process of asking "why" and looking deeper can work in your daily life as a student and well beyond as you strive to make good life decisions.

You also appreciate now that, regardless of your future occupation, solving significant problems of all types often requires collaboration and teamwork. Complex issues benefit from the input of people with a diversity of training, experience, and insight. In almost any career you will work with others to find the successful solutions to the challenges you face. Individuals you trust can prove essential for even personal problems you may face in the years ahead. Many successful people actually create their own personal "Board of Directors" to call on for advice when they make important decisions. We wish you a successful journey as you solve the challenges and investigations in your life. No life completely avoids stress and difficulty, but we hope some of the lessons you have learned in this introduction to medical investigation make you better able to make sound decisions. Thanks for allowing us into your life.

About the Authors

In his youth **Dr. Russ Hill** imagined himself playing professional baseball, encouraged by a successful high school baseball career. But higher levels of competition failed to ratify that expectation, so he had to pursue his backup plan. In college he trained for teaching, but upon graduation no jobs were open. Instead he found an opportunity in pharmaceutical sales. While doing that work he met a Podiatrist who was an alumnus of Dr. Hill's own high school. The doctor challenged him to further his science education and then apply to Podiatry school. He did and at the end of a career in health care he retired, still feeling the need for challenges in his life.

In pursuit of another challenge, Dr. Hill followed his daughter into the teaching profession, a profession he originally had pursued over twenty years earlier. Over the past decade and a half he has challenged his students to bump up their own aspirations, just as the Podiatrist had done for him. He still teaches middle school Science and STEM.

The current trend in education has put a focus on career readiness, and yet we have not seen a textbook that introduces students to medically-oriented careers. This one tries to do just that by providing insights into how doctors analyze problems and conduct medical investigations. Whether students end up with a medically oriented career or not, the analytical skills required of physicians have applications in almost all careers we expect to see opening up in the future. Besides, It never hurts to have some basic medical knowledge tucked away when collaborating with a physician to maintain your own good health.

Dr. Richard Griffith never imagined a career in medicine when he was your age. Instead electronics fascinated him at a time when America was very excited about going into outer space. He took math and physics in a small town high school from a former mining engineer who encouraged him to ask why, and challenge the simple answers to questions. In college he studied physics, but eventually recognized that his passion lay in solving everyday problems and not so much finding new sub-atomic particles. He went to graduate school in electrical engineering and got interested in medical applications for engineering tools. He got career guidance from an older engineer who had attended medical school and eventually became a researcher at the National Institutes of Health. Based on his advice, Griffith completed a doctorate in electrical engineering and then applied to medical school, frankly not expecting to get accepted since biology and chemistry were not a significant part of his prior studies. To his surprise they let him in and he managed to transition into this very different mode of thinking and learning.

His electrical engineering background got him involved in research in neurosurgery even before he finished medical school, but he decided that he needed a clinical specialty for a successful career, so he selected a residency in anesthesiology. That specialty seemed to best suit his array of interests. He since has done private practice, worked as a medical director in a major medical device company, and finally finished his career in academic medicine teaching medical students and resident physicians. Now retired in Vermont, he has been working to involve industrial designers more fully in the cause of Patient Safety, because mistakes in health care have become an alarmingly common occurrence despite the best intentions of health care professionals. It appears that industrial designers have some unique skills that may prove especially valuable in the future of safer medical care.

Russ Hill and Richard Griffith are First Cousins who grew up on opposite sides of this country, Griffith in Virginia and Hill in California. Griffith's Mother was the Sister of Hill's Father. Griffith was thirteen and Hill was eleven when they first met. Griffith's family had driven west for his Father to attend a summer workshop in economics and to visit their distant Hill relatives. They made that 6,000 miles round trip in the middle of summer with no radio or air conditioner in their car. Times were tough back then. The two cousins did not see one other in person again until seventeen years later when Hill's family visited the Griffith family in Virginia. In the ensuing years they have communicated by email as their friendship grew. They have gotten together a few times in New York, Montana, and Vermont, where Griffith now lives. In spite of the geographical barrier, they successfully collaborated by many e-mails for over a year in order to write this book.

Raella Hill married Russ more than 45 years ago, first meeting him in high school. She worked in hospitals before taking several years off to raise her two children. She then studied art and immersed herself in ceramics, photography, painting, and printmaking. Her final career job was as office manager for architectural photographers. Her interests now include her four grandchildren, printmaking, and yoga.

May all who gaze upon
this Certificate know--

has diligently and steadfastly
completed all the work
required to be known
now and for all time as
an official, certified
MEDICAL SCIENCE
INVESTIGATION 101
trained practitioner.

This official diploma and its conferred title is awarded by Dr's. Hill and Griffith without any authority given them by any organization or government, but is nonetheless well deserved by every student who has read Medical Science Investigation 101 and done all the assigned tasks in the accompanying workbook. Congratulations to you. Keep exercising your mind and working toward making this a better and safer world.

Made in the USA
Middletown, DE
16 November 2021